PSL MODEL RAILWAY GUIDE

1

Baseboards, Track and Electrification

Michael Andress

 Patrick Stephens, Cambridge

Softbound edition first published September 1979
Reprinted November 1981
Reprinted February 1983

Combined casebound edition (with *PSL Model
Railway Guide 2*) first published November 1981
Reprinted June 1982
Reprinted February 1983
Reprinted September 1983

ISBN 0-85059-358-1 (softbound)
ISBN 0-85059-587-8 (combined casebound)

Cover photograph by Brian Monaghan,
taken at the Wakefield Model Railway
Society.

Text photoset in 8 on 9pt Univers by
Stevenage Printing Limited, Stevenage.
Printed in Great Britain on 90 gsm Fineblade
coated cartridge and bound by The Garden
City Press, Letchworth, for the publishers
Patrick Stephens Limited, Bar Hill,
Cambridge, CB3 8EL, England.

Contents

4

Introduction

For many the first introduction to railway modelling is a train set. This is an excellent way to begin the hobby. Nowadays such sets are of very good quality in appearance, accuracy of scale and reliability of operation. Even though the simple train set can provide a great deal of enjoyment in setting up and running, particularly if extra track and points are added, it has many limitations. In time the enthusiast will probably want to progress to a more permanent model railway layout with its greater realism. This transitional phase is a very important stage in the hobby. A successful first layout may well encourage the modeller to go on in a pastime which can give him, or her, much pleasure and satisfaction over the years. Failure at this stage may lead to giving up the hobby altogether.

When building a layout it is tempting to rush ahead in an effort to get something running and to provide the structures and scenery which make a model railway interesting and attractive to look at. Though some more experienced modellers become especially interested in such aspects of the hobby as track construction, electrification and so on, for the beginner baseboard construction, track laying and wiring often seem rather dull and difficult jobs. They may be thought of as tasks to be done as quickly as possible so that one can get on to more exciting projects. Because of this and a lack of knowledge of the basic principles involved these jobs may be inadequately carried out. This is unfortunate as sound baseboard construction, accurate track laying and correct electrification and wiring are basic essentials in the building of a good model railway. By good, I mean one which will look and run well and which will give the enthusiast continuing pleasure and satisfaction.

If this work is not completed properly there can be recurrent problems and much time,

effort and additional expense may be involved in attempting to correct faults later. These difficulties may also spoil the enjoyment and cause dissatisfaction and disillusionment with the hobby.

My aim in this book is to provide the beginner with a straightforward guide to these important subjects. I make no claim to originality for the ideas presented here; they are based on the experience and ideas of many modellers and are, for the most part, standard practice. Indeed, this is not the place for experimental schemes or new, relatively untried innovations. The beginner will do much better to stick to well-tested methods.

Although, as I have suggested above, the principles described in this book are based on the work of many modellers, too many to credit individually, there are two whose ideas on baseboard construction are worthy of special mention. They are Cyril Freezer, now editor of *Model Railways*, who has done much to develop and popularise the basic grid form most often used in Britain, and Linn Westcott, formerly editor of the American magazine *Model Railroader*, who devised the excellent and ingenious 'L-Girder' system. Both these experts have also written extensively and with great clarity on model railway electrification.

I would like to thank all those modellers who have allowed me to use photographs of their models or layouts in this book. In particular I am indebted to Graham Bailey, Geoff Barlow, K.J. Churms, Howard Coulson, Paul Drombolis, Jim Gadd, Keith Gowen, P.D. Hancock, Brian Harrap, Terry Jenkins, Betty Kay, John Medd, Ron Prattley, Mike Sharman and Vernon Sparrow.

I am also grateful to those manufacturers who have helped me with information and photographs.

Baseboards

The baseboard is the foundation of a layout. Even though it is largely hidden on the completed model railway its importance should not be overlooked. Remember that if the baseboard proves to be defective you may have to scrap the whole layout and begin all over again!

Why do we need a baseboard?

It is perhaps a logical beginning to decide first of all why we need a baseboard at all. At one time train sets were usually 0 gauge, or even larger in size, and most often they were set out on the floor for use. This was fine as the large and robust track pieces were fairly resistant to accidental damage and much of the fun of laying out the line was to take it under and around the furniture, which in the imagination became tunnels, mountains, cuttings and so on. A few train sets are still made in the larger scales. The Triang Big Big Trains have been discontinued but the Lima, Timpo and LGB models are still available. These run very well on the floor and even out of doors in the garden. However, most train sets are now in 00 or smaller scales. The small size of the track sections in these scales means that care is needed when assembling the track, both to achieve proper alignment and to avoid damage and it is not really satisfactory to try to do this on the floor. There is also the danger that the track may be trodden on causing it to become bent, distorted or broken. The dust, dirt and fluff that collect on the floor will get into the motors and bearings of the locomotives and rolling stock, impairing their running. So in the smaller scales it is essential to work on a table or other surface. The usual choice is to set the railway up on a table—often the dining table. However, there are disadvantages. Often the table is needed for other purposes so that it may not always be available at the time when the operator wishes to set up the railway; or activities may have to be cut short so that the table can be used for a family meal. Another problem is

that the table may not be large enough. In 00 scale a reasonable sized table is needed to accommodate just the basic oval, and it is not often possible to add much further track unless the table is unusually large. Also there is always the risk of scratching or otherwise marking the table if, for example, a locomotive derails and damage of this sort will not make the enthusiast popular with the rest of the family if the table is an expensive piece of furniture.

Thus, the ideal arrangement even for a train set is to have a running surface provided specifically for it. Though you will probably want to progress eventually from your train set to a model railway layout there is no need to rush this. There is a good deal to be said for taking the time to try out various track arrangements with the train set track and with additional track sections and points purchased separately. Playing around with the train set in this way is enjoyable in itself and it is also very helpful in deciding what sort of track plan you would like for your first proper layout. To do this you will need a suitable surface on which to set up the track designs and even though you are not yet ready to start on a definitive layout there is no reason why you should not make up a baseboard for this purpose. If a suitable design is chosen it can be retained as the baseboard for the proper layout. It could be a rectangular board of appropriate size or the more flexible scheme of, say, four smaller baseboard sections which can be fitted together in various ways to form differently shaped baseboards. Whichever type is chosen it should be a solid top baseboard so that the track sections can be shuffled about as desired during the experimental stage.

For a train set it is convenient, as I have explained, to have a baseboard; for a model railway layout it is essential. The layout must be built up in a permanent form if it is to be properly developed, both operationally and scenically. Smooth running depends on the alignment of the track and the electrical

A train set can easily be developed into an interesting small layout when it is fitted on to a permanent baseboard. The layout shown here has track from a train set together with three points and some extra track purchased separately. The addition of a few structures and simple scenery completes the model railway.

A view of the underside of the baseboard for the layout in the previous picture, shown during construction. Because the baseboard top is chipboard, stronger and more rigid than wood fibre insulation board, less support is required and a simpler framing can be employed, as seen here, if you wish. However, if the layout is to be moved about frequently it is advisable to use the standard grid framing even with a chipboard top.

contacts; on a train set which is frequently set up and then dismantled fittings can become loosened or distorted which impairs operation. On a model railway layout the track is carefully and accurately aligned initially and then fixed in place so that it cannot move or become distorted. Good electrical connections can be made and maintained. With a temporary set-up the wiring must be kept simple but on a more permanent layout more complicated electrification is possible, permitting more in-

teresting and realistic control and operation. Last, but certainly not least, a permanent set-up is required before realistic scenic work can be carried out and this is essential for a complete model railway layout. Such a layout must have its own baseboard on which everything can be fixed. I have used the word permanent to distinguish a model railway layout from one which is set up afresh for each operating session and not to suggest or imply that a layout, once built, should never be changed. It is almost certain that you will want to alter or extend your railway from time to time. Eventually, with improving standards of modelling, changes in your interests or merely a desire to try something new you will most likely want to scrap your first layout and build another. If the original baseboard was of sound construction there is no reason why it should not be salvaged and reused for your new layout; if necessary being altered or extended for the purpose. Thus the work which you put into making a good baseboard to begin with will not be wasted.

Having decided that a baseboard is essential we can now consider our requirements. Obviously it must be flat and true when constructed. It should also be strong enough not to distort with time, changes in temperature and humidity, or with handling in the case of a portable layout. The baseboard must be rigid enough not to sag or bend from its own weight and sufficiently strong to take the weight of the operator leaning on or against it. Do not be misled into thinking that because you are modelling in N scale a flimsy base will be adequate. For the commonly used scales the weight of the models is insignificant and for the same size of board the construction must be as strong for an N-scale layout as for an 00-scale railway. However, it may be that because of the smaller size of the N-scale models and layout a smaller baseboard can be used and in that case lighter material may be adequate for the framing.

The choice of materials employed may also be influenced by the cost, availability and ease of construction. If the track is to be fixed down with pins, the top surface may be chosen so that these can be pushed into it easily.

The noise produced by the trains running is another factor to be considered and this is influenced to some extent by the materials used in the baseboard construction.

Commercial baseboards

Until recently anyone wanting a model railway baseboard had to build it himself or arrange to have one specially made. Now there are several ready-made boards available commercially. There are two very different types.

One is the base moulded in thick plastic or fibreglass. This type provides not only a base on which to fit the track but also a contoured terrain complete with hills, tunnels, rivers, roads and so on. This does, of course, restrict the design of the layout to one of the arrangements offered but it is a way of completing a scenic model railway layout with an absolute minimum of time and effort.

A variety of baseboards with different track and scenic features are made in 00/HO, N and Z scales by Kibri, Noch, Hornby and DAS, and some of these offer possibilities for extension or combination to produce larger layouts. Most of the bases are pre-coloured and some of the Kibri and Noch boards even have grassy areas represented by flocking. To give greater strength wooden framing is fitted into the Kibri and Noch bases. For the most part the preformed bases are intended for use on a table or other support but the Kibri baseboards have provision for fitting legs which are available as separate items. The moulded bases have the advantage of making it very quick and easy to provide a scenic setting for the train set but they are rather expensive and there is little scope for the modeller to create his own individual layout.

The other form of baseboard available commercially is of the standard type frequently constructed by enthusiasts for their own layouts but provided ready-made or in kit form. This is very convenient but will naturally be more expensive than building your own from scratch. Baseboards of this type are offered by Raitab, Alan Borwell and Puffers. The boards are modular baseboards and can be fitted together as required to give the size and shape wanted for your layout. The bases from Puffers are 4 ft × 2 ft; the other manufacturers offer them in a selection of sizes up to 4 ft × 2 ft. The Raitab baseboards, for example, have wooden framing and legs with metal fittings; the kits are available with or without tops of chipboard or Sundeala as desired.

Faller have recently introduced kits for baseboards and legs of wooden construction with a top surface of re-inforced corrugated board.

Materials

For the modeller who wishes to construct his own baseboard we should now look at the various materials which can be used. Methods of construction will be considered in detail later but a baseboard is essentially a frame or grid with or without a covering top and these two parts are conveniently discussed separately.

Many different materials have been tried for the framing but wood is by far the most commonly employed and is the only one we need consider here. Most modellers will need to use softwood; hardwood has the advantage of greater strength but is more

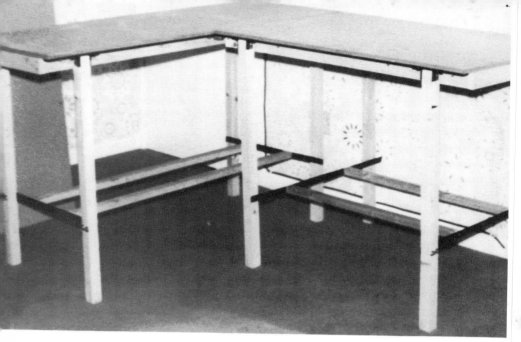

difficult to work and these days tends to be expensive. Sometimes it is possible to obtain old timber cheaply from demolition sites and other sources and provided the wood is free from wood-worm or rot there is the advantage that it will be well seasoned. Usually, however, the enthusiast will have to buy softwood from a local timber yard or DIY shop and this will be perfectly satisfactory. As far as possible choose pieces which are straight, without bends or twists and are free from cracks or large knots. Nowadays the wood will not have been properly seasoned and if there is time it is a good idea to let the timber stand in the house for a few weeks before use, especially if you have central heating. This will allow the wood to shrink before it is made up into a baseboard rather than afterwards when this might cause warping.

The most frequently used size of timber is a nominal 2 in × 1 in, with an actual finished size of 1⅞ in × ⅞ in, but other sizes may also be needed depending on the type and dimensions of the baseboard. Fixing is with wood screws, 1½ or 2 in No 8 flathead are the most useful sizes and white glue such as Gloy.

For the top surface, if one is required, there is a wider choice of materials. These vary in strength and rigidity, weight and cost and the individual modeller should choose the one which best suits his own requirements.

Wood fibre insulation board ½ in thick is very popular. It is cheap, easy to cut with a saw or knife and takes pins and track spikes without difficulty. This material must be

An L-shaped baseboard made up from Raitab baseboard table kits showing the neat construction of these units. The kits are available in a range of sizes from 3 ft × 1 ft to 4 ft × 2 ft and can be combined to form any required size and shape of baseboard. (Photo courtesy of Raitab.)

supported at intervals not greater than a foot to prevent sagging. It is relatively light and has good, sound deadening properties. A useful alternative is Sundeala which is harder and stronger but also more expensive.

Chipboard is another frequently used material. It is stronger and more rigid than the insulation board and requires less bracing, making it useful for portable layouts. The cost and weight are greater and it is also noisier than the wood fibre board. Because it is much harder it is more difficult to work and will not take fine pins or track spikes as they tend to bend instead of pushing in easily.

Plywood was popular and is still often used in the United States, where I suspect it may be less expensive than here. Some saving can be made by using ply with a good finish on one side only and fitting it with the poorer surface underneath on to the framing while the better side forms the top face of the baseboard. Plywood is also more difficult to work than the insulation board and it is quite noisy.

Blockboard is another alternative material. It is rigid but expensive and heavy. It might be worthwhile employing it in areas where rigidity is important and it is not convenient to add extra bracing. For example it could be

Sturdy baseboard construction on a large exhibition layout. Chipboard has been used as the baseboard top and also as the track base for the tracks above baseboard level.

used as the base for a goods yard on a higher level with limited clearance beneath for low level tracks making it impossible to fit bracing.

Hardboard is mentioned only to be dismissed as quite unsuitable. It tends to warp, buckle and distort even when well braced, causing problems with any track laid on it. It is also noisy and the surface is too hard for pins and track spikes to be pushed in without drilling holes first.

Tools

Fortunately only a simple tool kit is needed for baseboard construction and anyone with an interest in carpentry or DIY work will almost certainly have a more than adequate selection of tools already.

For cutting the frame pieces to size and possibly for cutting the baseboard top a saw will be required. A handsaw is perfectly adequate and a tenon saw is a good choice as this will be ideal for making neat joints. A mitre block is helpful in keeping the cuts square and accurate so that the pieces will fit properly together. I have a Copydex 'Joint-master' which is very useful as it enables one to make all types of joints easily and accurately. It is by no means essential but is well worth while considering as an extra item of equipment, particularly if you are planning a large layout or if you do other woodwork as well.

A power saw is also something of a luxury item and is certainly not necessary, though again might be worth purchasing if you plan a large baseboard or if it will be useful to you for other projects as well. The circular saw type is good for the construction of baseboard framing, particularly of the 'L-Girder' type whereas a sabre saw can save a great deal of time if you wish to use the so-called 'cookie cutter' method of baseboard fabrication or for cutting track bases.

Baseboard framing can be made up very satisfactorily using only butt joints but you may prefer to make halved joints and if so you will need a chisel for cutting away the waste wood between the saw cuts. Assembly of the frame will be with screws, so suitable holes must be drilled to take them. For a small layout a hand drill is all that is required but for a larger layout where many holes will be needed you might think it worth buying a power drill. Drill bits to suit the sizes of screws you will use, together with a countersink, are also necessary. It may be most convenient to buy a set of drill bits so that it is easy to drill holes of any size when needed. To fix and tighten the screws a screwdriver will be required; make sure you get one of the appropriate size as too small a blade will damage the slots in the screwheads and the screws will be difficult to tighten or to remove. If you have a power drill you can buy a screwdriver bit to fit into it and this will speed up fixing the screws very considerably. This is not of much consequence on a small layout but can save a lot of time on a large one. A steel rule and a square should also form part of the tool set for marking out before cutting and for checking during assembly.

If insulation board is used as the top surface of the baseboard some people prefer to cut it with a knife rather than a saw as this is less messy, producing much less dust. An ordinary modelling knife is not suitable; a stronger larger knife is needed. The Stanley knife is ideal and this useful tool will also come in handy for many other hobby jobs where the usual modelling knife is not heavy or strong enough. When insulation board is employed for the baseboard surface it is most conveniently fixed onto the frame with nails so a hammer should be included in the tool kit.

For cleaning up the cut edges of the frame and top I use a Surform followed by a file and sandpaper.

Another piece of equipment which is not essential but which I have found extremely useful is a Black & Decker 'Workmate'. This is in effect a combined workbench and large vice or clamp and it folds up for easy storage and carrying. The 'Workmate' makes it easy to hold long pieces of wood for sawing, drilling, filing and other work without needing anyone else to help. It is invaluable for many jobs around the home as well as in layout construction.

In modern houses and flats particularly it is often difficult to find somewhere to carry out the work involved in building a layout baseboard. To achieve good results most easily a clean, well lit area is desirable. In good weather the work can be done out of doors if necessary but railway modelling is most often undertaken in the winter when bad weather and the dark evenings may make this impracticable. The garage, if you have one, is an alternative but it may be cramped when the car is in it and often the lighting is inadequate. A workshop or workroom is the ideal but few of us are fortunate enough to have a room which can be devoted to this purpose. Though it may seem an unlikely choice of site I find the best place to work on a project of this type is the kitchen. The lighting is good and the floor is tiled so there is no difficulty in sweeping up the sawdust and wood shavings. Provided care is taken to do no damage and the room is properly cleaned up afterwards a small layout baseboard can be constructed here without difficulty or undue disruption. But do not

The framing for a 4 ft × 1 ft 9 in baseboard section showing typical grid construction using butt and halved joints. The modeller has fitted the end joists to the ends of the side girders; a stronger frame would have resulted if these joists had been placed between the girders.

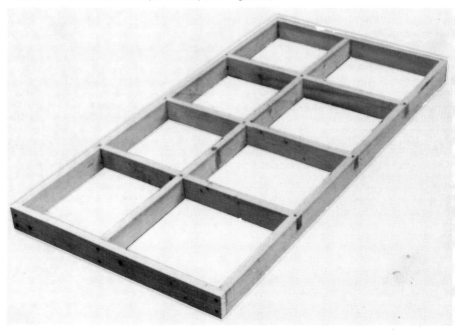

forget to check that the kitchen is not needed for cooking or other domestic activities at the time you want to use it!

Baseboard size

There are many factors which may influence the size and type of baseboard chosen. The size and shape of the layout, where it will be located, whether it is to be a permanent fixture, semi-permanent or portable, plans for future modifications and extensions and personal preferences must all be taken into account. I recommend most strongly that a beginner's first layout should be kept small and simple, even if it is designed to permit later extension. There are several good reasons for this. First of all, there are various construction techniques and methods to be mastered and it is much easier, quicker and cheaper to learn these on a small layout where the amount of work required is relatively limited. In a small area progress seems more rapid, encouraging the modeller to carry on. A model railway does not need to be large and complex to be enjoyable to construct and operate. Indeed, the beginner who tackles too ambitious a layout will find construction and, if he ever completes the model, maintenance so time consuming that he may have little time left to enjoy running it.

Even with a small layout it is worth considering whether to make the baseboard in one piece or as two or more sections which are then joined together, either on a more or less permanent basis or temporarily for operating sessions if the layout is to be portable. There is a natural tendency when going on from a train set to a model railway to think in terms of an oval track plan on a baseboard about 6 ft × 4 ft in size, the board then being built as a single unit. Though the plan may not look very big on paper as a small scale plan, a baseboard of this size is surprisingly large, heavy and difficult to carry, particularly as on the finished layout one side of it is covered with fragile scenery and structures. However, for convenience in construction, layouts up to about this size which are not likely to be moved about frequently can be satisfactorily built on a single baseboard. A layout with a length no greater than 6 ft can be carried end up through a doorway and this makes it much more movable than if it is any longer.

For larger layouts, even if the need to move them is not anticipated, it is worth while arranging construction so that the baseboard can be taken apart into smaller units without damaging the layout unduly. If the modeller has to move house or wishes to show the

layout at an exhibition it is then possible to transport it. There is also the bonus that smaller units may be more convenient to construct in the beginning, especially if one has to resort to working on the kitchen table!

A portable layout must obviously be small enough, or break down into units which are sufficiently small, for easy handling and transportation. An ideal size for these sections is 4 ft × 2 ft. This is small enough for easy handling by one person, yet large enough that the number of separate units required to make up the layout is not excessive. The individual modeller may, however, decide to make his units a different size, perhaps because of the size or shape of his layout or so that the sections will fit into his car for transportation, or into a large cupboard for storage. The sections need not be the same in size or shape but the use of a standard module can be advantageous both in construction and in storage.

We will look at the construction of these layout sections and methods of fitting them together later in the book.

Baseboard height

There is no 'correct' height for a model railway layout; everyone has his own ideas on the best level for the baseboard. The height chosen may depend on whether the model is to be operated by an adult, a child or both. Because model railways appear more realistic if viewed at about eye level, rather than from above, a position above the normal table level is usually preferred for the baseboard. Conversely it is easier to operate the layout if you have an overall view from above the layout; this is most important on a complicated layout. One compromise solution is to choose the height so that the layout is at about eye level for spectators sitting in low chairs, while the operator has a high stool so that he can see the whole layout easily.

The width of the layout is also relevant in deciding how high it should stand. The greatest easy reach across a layout is when it is at about waist height so this is the level to choose if the layout is wider than 18-24 in.

The baseboard may need to be high up to clear furniture or other items in the room. If it must be high a narrow scenic layout is the most suitable type.

Most layouts are between about 36 and 48 in from the floor with an average of perhaps 42 in. There are some exceptions to the general rules on baseboard height. Coffee table layouts, for example, will of course be quite low, typically about 18 in high. Portable layouts should not be much more than 3 ft high because they would be unstable.

Baseboard construction

Having considered some general points regarding baseboards we can now look at the methods of building them. There are several different types of baseboard construction.

Basic frame or grid

This is the standard form of baseboard construction. The frame is usually made up from 2 in × 1 in timber (these are nominal sizes and the actual dimensions of the finished wood is 1⅞ in × ⅞ in). The main side girders are cut to run the length of the board and they will be braced by joists fitted across between them at intervals not greater than 12 in. Note that the end joists must also be fitted between the main girders and not on to their ends as this gives greater strength. To join the girders and joists simple butt joints with two screws and glue are perfectly adequate though halved joints may be used if you prefer.

For baseboards up to a foot wide no central girder is required but above this width one is needed for each extra foot width. Halved joints are usually employed where these girders cross the joists but these can be

avoided if you wish by staggering the joists so that butt joints can be used.

The method of construction is the same whether you are building, for example, a 6 ft × 4 ft baseboard as a single unit, or as three 4 ft × 2 ft boards which will be fitted together to form a 6 ft × 4 ft base, but there will be some duplication of the girders in the latter arrangement and therefore more material will be needed. Sometimes a baseboard which is not rectangular or square may be needed, perhaps an L-shape or a rectangle with arms extending from it. The simplest method is to build it as two or more rectangular bases which are fitted together to produce the desired form. Take care in assembling the basic frame as it must have a perfectly flat upper surface to take the baseboard top.

If the baseboard is to be made up of two or more smaller units provision must be made for these to be fixed together firmly and accurately. For a permanent layout a convenient method is to bolt the two sections together with coach bolts. To ensure an accurate fit, clamp the two baseboard units firmly together making sure the two pieces are perfectly aligned and then drill through both at once. When clamping them pay special attention to the top surfaces as there must be no step where they

Basic grid for 4 ft × 2 ft layout section made up from 2 in × 1 in timber. Construction employs halved joints for central girder and butt joints elsewhere; if preferred butt joints could be used throughout by staggering the joists at either side of the central girder.

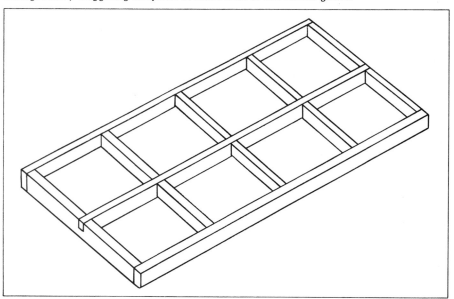

An L-shaped baseboard shown from the underside so the 2 in × 1 in wood framing is visible. Note how the L-shaped board has been made up from two rectangular units, one 4 ft × 1 ft and the other 2 ft × 1 ft. The two have been screwed together and a metal angle has been used for strengthening. The baseboard top is ½ in thick wood fibre insulation board.

join and no twisting of one in relation to the other.

Though the track bases and scenery supports can be fitted on to the frame directly (the open top or open frame baseboard system) the beginner is best advised to fit a top surface on to the basic frame (the solid top form of baseboard).

Solid top baseboards

The material employed for the top surface can be any of those listed in the section on materials earlier in the book. One of the most frequently used is ½ in thick wood fibre insulation board. As previously mentioned this is relatively soft and easy to work, inexpensive and takes pins and spikes easily but must be supported at intervals no greater than 12 ins to avoid sagging. After cutting to size, a top of insulation board should be nailed and glued on to the frame. Another popular choice for the top surface is chipboard. This is stronger and more rigid than the insulation board but is heavier, more expensive and harder to work. A top of this material is fixed down by screwing and gluing. The greater strength and rigidity of chipboard means that it needs less support then the insulation board and on small layouts lighter framing can be used if desired.

The solid top type of baseboard uses more material than the open top method but has the advantage of simplicity. The presence of a complete top surface also means that the modeller can use the baseboard to lay out the track in various arrangements before he decides on a final plan. Then, wherever he wishes to lay the tracks there will be support. It also makes it easy to alter the position of tracks if you change your mind during construction about the layout plan you want.

A disadvantage is that it is more awkward to build a layout with tracks at various levels, particularly if tracks below the level of the baseboard surface are required. Elevated tracks can be carried on a track base cut from chipboard or ply supported by wood blocks fixed on to the baseboard top. If you wish, the track base can be surfaced with insulation board to allow easy insertion of track pins and to reduce noise. Cyril Freezer has described a neat way of giving a smooth start to a rising track where it leaves the main baseboard level. He suggests cutting a tongue of the insulation board top surface and packing it up to the required grade. This tongue then leads smoothly on to the track base which is supported as described above.

If there must be tracks below the level of the baseboard top then this and possibly part of the baseboard framing must be cut away in this area. Alternatively if the baseboard is made up of separate sections joined together these may be planned so that low level tracks can be carried down between two of these sections. Either way such complications are best avoided, particularly by the beginner. If you want to construct a layout with tracks on multiple levels the most suitable type of baseboard is the open top form, either a basic grid frame or an L-girder frame. This should be designed so that the lowest level tracks run on track bases fitted directly on to the surface of the frame and the other tracks and scenery are then built upwards from the base.

If a deep valley or ravine is wanted, part of the baseboard can be dropped down to accommodate it—the area being strengthened with wood bracing or by metal brackets. A convenient arrangement is to

Baseboards

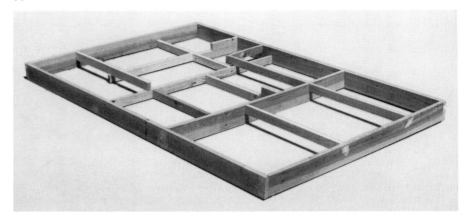

Baseboard for a 6 ft × 4 ft layout during construction. 4 in × 1 in timber was used for part of the framing and 2 in × 1 in for the rest. This has produced an area 2 in below the general ground level for a lake and river to be modelled. An additional joist at the right-hand end of the layout should have been provided to give better support for the top.

Later, during the construction, part of the wood fibre insulation board top has been fitted after cutting it to shape for one side of the lake and river. Further pieces of insulation board will be fixed in place to form the ground at this side and, between and at a lower level, to form a basis for the lake and river.

have the dropped section between two baseboard units.

Open-top baseboards

With this system a top surface is applied over the open frame only where it is needed for tracks or for features such as an industrial or urban area. This method uses less material and gives more flexibility in planning tracks and scenery at varying levels; it is particularly

suitable for hilly or mountainous scenery. The track bases are cut from chipboard or ply and faced with insulation board as for the elevated tracks in the solid top method. However, these track bases are supported directly on the framing of the baseboard. For higher level tracks the track bases are carried on risers, wood strips fixed on to the framing and extending up to the required height.

The lack of a flat surface on which to lay

A baseboard section of the open-frame type. Note the track base supported by risers. The gap in the centre is where a large bridge spanning a gorge will be fitted. Note also the scenery supports built up from wood and hardboard.

out the track while planning and building the layout makes things more difficult especially for the beginner. One solution is to fit a top surface temporarily and to plan the track arrangement out full size on this. Once the track plan has been finalised the top is removed and the track locations are transferred to the frame for positioning the track bases and risers.

Model Railroader magazine staff devised a rather ingenious method, descriptively named the 'cookie cutter' technique, which combines the simplicity of the solid top with some of the flexibility of the open top system when it comes to adding high level trackage.

The 'cookie cutter'

The framing, of conventional type, is covered with a flat top of plywood which is screwed but not glued down. The surface is used to lay out the track in various ways until the final arrangement is decided on. If desired the tracks can be fixed down at this stage provided care is taken not to cover any of the screws which are holding the top down. The beginner can thus complete a simple one level layout which he can enjoy operating. This can be accomplished quickly and easily as in the solid top system. Later the modeller may wish to make the layout more interesting by introducing different levels for the tracks. If a track, either a new one to be added or one of the tracks already present, is to be elevated, saw cuts are made through the plywood top at either side of the track, taking care not to cut through any of the joists. Any screws holding this strip are removed and the strip and track are raised to the required height. Wood risers are fitted to support it. Though the technique is said to work well even with tracks already laid being raised up, there would seem to be a risk of such tracks being distorted unless this is done very carefully. However, the method does offer the benefits of easy planning and being able to get the trains running without delay, together with the potential for further development later. As the scenic side progresses part of the baseboard top can be cut away to enable the modelling of rivers, lakes and valleys.

L-Girder Framework

Some years ago Linn Westcott, who was editor of the American *Model Railroader* magazine at the time, devised an excellent new form of open frame baseboard with many important advantages. This is the 'layer' method and the essential feature is that the joists rest on top of the girders instead of lying between them. The main longitudinal girders are usually made L-shaped for greater strength and for convenience in the fixing of joists, risers and other parts to them. Therefore this type of framework is usually known as the 'L-Girder Frame'. The system was originally designed for large permanent layouts and each girder was built up by screwing and gluing a strip of 2 in × 1 in wood along the edge of a 4 in × 2 in plank to form a girder which was L-shaped in cross section. For smaller layouts or modular baseboards the girders can be lighter; 2 in × ½ in and 2 in × 1 in wood is suitable. If a circular saw bench is available L-girders can be cut very quickly and easily. Just two cuts with the saw into a wood strip will leave an L-girder and the piece removed from inside the L can be used as joists. The L-girders are very strong and convenient but are not essential and on a small layout simple girders can be used satisfactorily if preferred.

The important feature of the system is the position of the joists on top of the girders and this gives several advantages. The joists do not have to be cut accurately, as they must be in the basic grid to fit between the girders, so construction is simpler. Because all the screws are fitted from below they remain accessible and are easy to remove, making alterations and extensions to the layout much simpler than with the more conventional framework. Joists can be moved easily either to get them out of the way or to provide support when changes are made to tracks or scenery and the whole system is very flexible. The L-girder framework gives the maximum strength and therefore needs less material than other framing, making it lighter and cheaper to build. It is usually employed as an open-top baseboard and its versatility makes it ideal for layouts with tracks at multiple levels and correspondingly uneven scenic terrain. However, it is also perfectly satisfactory for a small beginner's layout with a solid top fitted on to a simple L-girder frame.

With this system the legs are not placed at the ends of the layout or layout section. The strongest position for the legs is where the long girders are crossed by joists and the best location is about 1/5 of the way in from the front, rear and ends. Legs placed here are also less likely to be accidentally knocked than ones in the conventional positions. 2 in × 1 in or 2 in square timber is used for the legs and these must be braced. This bracing should be at about 45° and reach to within 6 in of the floor at the lower end for maximum steadiness.

Baseboard support

On a permanent free-standing layout legs cut from 2 in square timber can be fixed into the corners of the baseboard frame with screws and braced either with wood struts or with metal angle brackets. To make sure the baseboard top will be level clamp the legs in place with 'C' clamps and set the whole thing up on a flat floor. Put a shallow dish filled with water on top of the baseboard and adjust the legs until the top is perfectly level as shown by the water. Tighten up the clamps and keep them on until you have drilled the holes for the screws fixing the legs. On longer baseboards, legs will be needed at 4 ft intervals. If the layout is semi-permanent only and must be taken down from time to time, bolts rather than screws should be used to fix the legs in place. Fitting wing nuts on to the bolts instead of the ordinary nuts will make them easier to remove.

Model Railway Guide 1

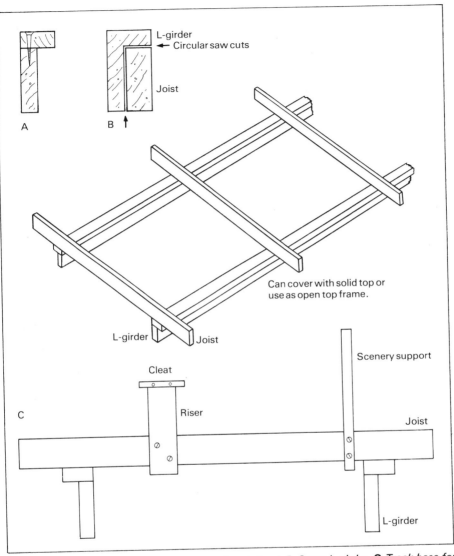

*L-girder framing. **A** Built up L-girder screwed and glued. **B** Sawn L-girder. **C** Track base for elevated track fixed to cleat (left) and for non-elevated track supported directly on joists (right).*

A beginner's layout is most often made as a free standing unit even if it will be placed against the wall. However, if there is no objection to plugging the wall, the rear of the baseboard can be supported by a batten or brackets of wood or metal fixed on to the wall. If the layout is a narrow one designed to be fitted along the wall or walls of the room it may be possible to support it entirely by fixing it, shelf-like, to the wall. However, most layouts are too wide for this and will also require legs to support the front edge.

It may be convenient to use furniture (a table, chest of drawers, low cupboard or bookcase) to support the layout rather than fitting it with legs of its own. You may have suitable pieces of furniture already; felt pads may be needed between the layout and the

Baseboards

A sturdy, but simply made, trestle used for layout support.

Jim Gadd's attractive 4 mm scale 9 mm gauge model railway layout has been constructed as a number of separate easily transported sections making it completely portable. It has been shown at numerous exhibitions. The photograph shows a passenger train arriving at Moulsett station.

top surface of the furniture to prevent scratching. Alternatively you can often buy secondhand furniture cheaply and you may find some useful items this way. If you make any repairs necessary and repaint the pieces of furniture they can be made very presentable and there may be drawers or shelves which will be useful for storing rolling stock and other models. Another source of furniture which can be used to support a layout is the whitewood range of ready-made and kit items; several matching units can be selected and used for a layout along one wall.

Another way of supporting a layout is to use trestles. These can be fixed or folding trestles and can be of quite simple construction.

Portable layouts

A portable layout must break down easily into units or modules small enough to be transported and stored without difficulty. It is best to design it so that it can be assembled, dismantled and moved by one person working alone. This means that the owner need not rely on anyone else for assistance. As it may well be necessary to set up and take down the layout for every operating session this should be arranged to take as little time as possible. When not in use the layout must

be stored away, preferably neatly and safe from dust and accidental damage.

The sections or modules for a portable layout can be fabricated following the usual methods of construction. A grid frame of 2 in × 1 in wood with a top surface of insulation board or chipboard is suitable. The size of each module should certainly not be greater than 4 ft × 2 ft and units 3 ft long and 12-18 in wide may well be better. For these smaller sections 1 in square timber is adequate particularly if chipboard is used for the top of the baseboard. The small units are more convenient to transport in a car and are small enough to be stored in a large cupboard. The sections of a layout need not be identical in size and shape, but there are some advantages in having a standard module. Construction may be faster and easier because they can be mass produced and storage is likely to be simpler if all the modules are uniform. A neat method of storage is to construct a cupboard of the appropriate size to take the modules sliding on to supporting ledges fitted inside each end of the cupboard, very much as if they were drawers in a chest.

To fix the units together coach bolts can be used as with a permanent layout, preferably fitting the bolts with wing nuts to make

Part of a large N-scale layout built by Graham Bailey. The first section, to the right of the picture, is supported on two trestles. Further sections, one of which is shown here, are bolted on and each has one pair of legs at one end, the other end being supported by the trestle or legs of the adjacent section. These additional sections are fitted at both ends of the first unit.

assembly quicker and easier. Unfortunately with setting up and dismantling the layout repeatedly the holes become worn larger so that the bolts are a loose fit and alignment of the sections may not be exact. One solution to this problem is to fit pieces of metal pipe, or tube of appropriate inside diameter, into the holes so that the bolts bear on the metal and do not enlarge the holes. However, an even better method has been suggested by Cyril Freezer. He uses cast brass flapback hinges with the pins removed and replaced with round nails of suitable size with the upper part bent to form handles. The adjacent baseboard sections are clamped together so that they are accurately aligned and the hinges are fixed on with one flap on each side of the join. When the pin is removed the two sections can be taken apart. The two hinge halves make it easy to line up the sections for fitting together again and when the pins are fitted into the hinges at each end of the join the two boards will be held firmly together.

You may find it convenient to make a portable layout so that adjacent units form identical pairs. Each pair can then be hinged together to form a double unit which folds up on itself; this provides protection during transportation and storage. The hinges must be mounted on blocks well above track level to provide clearance for structures and scenery, which should be arranged to interlock so that they do not clash when the module is folded up.

Portable layouts are often supported on furniture or trestles when in use. If legs are needed it is convenient to have them hinged on to the underside of the baseboards and to fit metal braces to lock them in position when the layout is erected. Usually only one module, the largest if they vary in size, needs to have four legs; the others will be fitted with a pair of legs at one end while the other end is supported by the next baseboard section.

If insulation board is used as the top surface for a portable layout it is desirable to fit a facing strip of ½ in square stripwood to protect the soft insulation board at the ends of the baseboard. Firm fixation for the rails of the tracks crossing the baseboard joins is achieved by soldering them to the heads of screws in this wood strip.

When arranging storage for the sections of a portable layout remember that the locomotives and rolling stock may have to be removed from the railway when it is not in use and that suitable storage must also be provided for them.

Lifting sections

If a layout fitted along a wall crosses the door of the room some means of access must be provided. If the layout is fairly high it may be possible to duck under it but a more satisfactory arrangement is to have a lifting section of the baseboard at this point. This is, in effect, merely a small baseboard section constructed in the usual manner. You may prefer to use chipboard rather than insulation board for the top surface to give greater rigidity to the lifting piece. The section is hinged at one end using ordinary flapback hinges mounted on wooden blocks at least an inch thick. A 2 in × 1 in strip of wood is fixed along the lower edge of the adjacent baseboard at the other side of the gap to support the end of the lifting section when it is in the down position.

Foldaway baseboards

Few modellers are lucky enough to have a room which can be devoted entirely to their hobby; usually the model railway layout must be fitted into one of the ordinary rooms in the house and should interfere as little as possible with the other uses of the room. One way in which this may be accomplished is to make a baseboard which is hinged or pivoted at one edge so that it folds up against the wall when not in use. Many successful layouts of this type have been built ranging from small N-scale railways which fold up into a bookcase or cupboard to a complete 8 ft × 10 ft HO scale layout, constructed by an American enthusiast, which swings up to form a false wall right across one end of his dining room. This layout takes up only a 26 in wide strip across the room when it is not in use!

The best arrangement is to build a wall unit, complete with shelves and/or cupboards if desired, and to fix this firmly to the wall. The baseboard is then supported from this. A small layout can be hinged on to it but a large layout is better pivoted on lengths of steel rod in metal bearing tubes. On large layouts, counterweights to balance the layout make it easier and safer to raise or lower the baseboard.

There are several points to be remembered with a foldaway layout. When the operating session is over, all the locomotives and rolling stock must, of course, be removed before the baseboard is folded up; it is convenient to include storage accommodation for them in the wall unit. Proper catches or bolts are essential to prevent the layout from dropping down accidentally.

Note that on a hinged layout there is no

access from the rear edge. Therefore on any baseboard wider than 3 ft it is preferable to have a central operating and access well. The layout can be arranged so that the front edge is supported by furniture such as a chest of drawers or a table when the baseboard is down, or it can be fitted with folding or detachable legs. Since raising and lowering the baseboard imposes additional strain on it, rather thicker material than usual may be preferred for the framing.

Coffee table layouts

The introduction of the very small scales, 009, N and Z, has enabled the construction of an interesting operating model railway layout in a very small space. Some modellers have taken advantage of this to build small layouts into coffee tables. These are very convenient to operate and, of course, there is no problem of storage; when nicely finished these layouts form attractive pieces of furniture and they certainly stimulate interest and conversation amongst visitors.

Typically a layout will be about 3 ft × 2 ft or 18 in in size with a continuous track plan, either an oval or a figure of eight design. The base and sides are often of ½ in thick plywood, with or without a frame of 2 in × 1 in timber beneath the base. The top is made

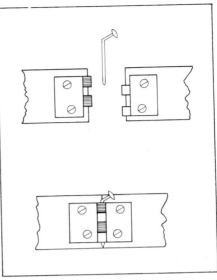

The hinge method of joining baseboard sections. Pin of hinge is removed and hinge halves fitted to baseboard sections. To join the two units, hinge halves are aligned and a round nail of appropriate size is used to hold them together.

Baseboard construction for the coffee table layout built by K.J. Churms. A box-like unit was made up from ½-in ply fixed with 1½-in No 8 screws and nails. Angle brackets inside the front corners provide greater rigidity. (Diagram by K.J. Churms.)

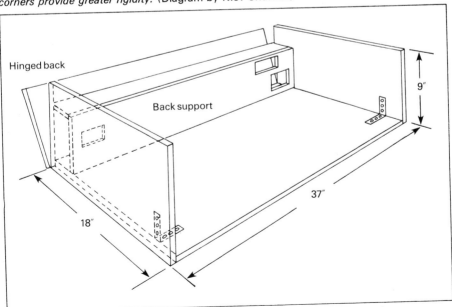

Hinged back

Back support

9″

37″

18″

Baseboards

An attractive coffee table layout built by K.J. Churms. The 009 layout measures 3 ft ˅ 18 in and has a twisted figure of eight track plan giving a good length of run. (Photo courtesy K.J. Churms).

from plate glass so that the layout can be viewed while also being used as a coffee table. Sometimes the sides are also made of plate glass. Ready-made legs in a variety of styles and materials are available from DIY shops and only require screwing into place on the underside of the baseboard. In keeping with their use as coffee tables the layouts are quite low, with the top perhaps 18 in above the floor. This also helps to make them more stable and steady.

An alternative method of construction was used by the MAP staff some years ago when they built a layout of this type which was featured in *Model Railway News* magazine. They used ¾ in square steel Dexion Speedframe tubes and joiners to make the frame with a baseboard of ½ in thick blockboard and a top of plate glass. Wooden dowels fitted across the frame below the baseboard formed a convenient rack for magazines. The finished model was a very neat piece of furniture.

Bookcase layouts

The lounge is a pleasant place in which to operate a model railway. The room is usually warm and comfortable and one can be sociable with the rest of the family while enjoying the hobby. The coffee table layout is one way in which a layout can be fitted into the lounge in an acceptable form but the scope of such a model is limited even in the very small scales and the idea is not really feasible for 00 scale.

An alternative is to incorporate a layout into some other piece of furniture. The modern style of wall units show considerable potential for a scheme of this sort, particularly if the modeller can design and build the units himself to suit his railway modelling requirements. If the finished piece of furniture is to be acceptable for the lounge the general workmanship and finish must be good and some ability at woodwork is needed for successful construction. There

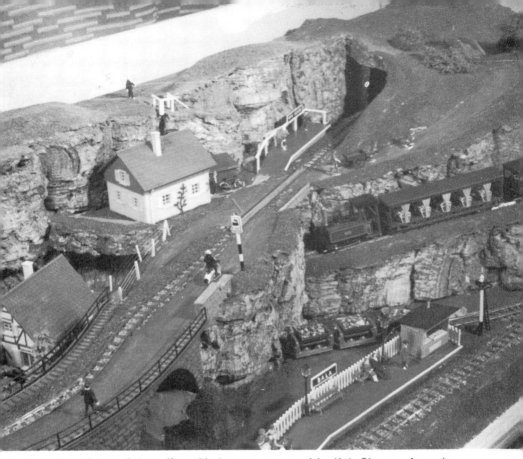

A closer view of part of the coffee table layout constructed by K.J. Churms. Attractive scenery makes the layout appear larger than it is. (Photo courtesy K.J. Churms.)

are quite a number of kits and ready-made units which can be fitted together in various combinations now available and the modeller may be able to utilise some of these if he does not feel capable of building the whole thing from scratch.

Ideally the layout should be covered when not in use both to protect it from dust and damage and to keep it out of sight when the lounge is used for other activities. However it should be possible to get it ready for operation with a minimum of effort. The modeller can also take the opportunity to include shelves and cupboards for general use or to accommodate books, magazines and other model railway items.

Ron Prattley has built a fine unit of this type, an attractive bookcase in which the layout is completely hidden when not in use. For operation the layout is revealed by removing the bookcase top; this itself forms a further section of the layout when it is

reversed and fitted on to the end of the bookcase. The layout is completed by the addition of the fiddle yard which is stored in the bookcase at other times. Ron built the bookcase from pine and he used self-adhesive plastic over this to give an excellent finished appearance as can be seen in the accompanying pictures.

Vernon Sparrow is another modeller who has been able to fit his layout into the lounge. He has constructed a shelf along one wall above the furniture to carry his model railway; a neat appearance has been achieved by making the shelf match the furniture.

There are a number of shelving systems designed for home assembly, available from DIY shops and the modeller could arrange one of these to provide neatly finished shelves, one for a narrow layout and others for books, magazines and models.

Baseboards

Above Ron Prattley built this superb bookcase to house his 00-scale layout in his lounge. When not in use the model railway is completely covered keeping it safe from damage and dust. **Below** For operation the top of the bookcase is removed, reversed and added onto the end of the bookcase to extend the layout. The fiddle yard (above large shelf in bookcase) has yet to be put in place at the end of the layout. (Photos by Ron Prattley.)

Above *Vernon Sparrow built this neatly finished shelf matching the other units of furniture which he also constructed, to support his 00-scale layout along one wall of his lounge. The layout is seen here from the usual viewpoint. Although the shelf is only 16½ in wide an interesting track layout has been featured (see track plan).* **Below** *This view shows the layout as seen from an armchair.* (Photos courtesy Vernon Sparrow.)

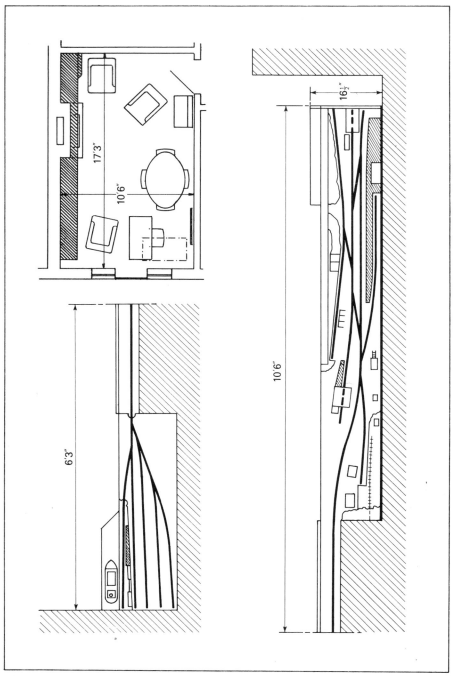

Above *Layout plan for Vernon Sparrow's 00-scale layout together with a plan of his lounge showing how the layout has been fitted into the room.* (Plans courtesy of Vernon Sparrow.)

Model Railway Guide 1

Track

Much of the appeal of railway modelling is that a layout is not merely a static collection of models built or purchased by the enthusiast but is a miniature working replica of the real railways. To enjoy a layout to the full it is essential that it should work well and realistically. The track is fundamental to this and every effort should be made to lay it accurately. If an item of rolling stock runs badly it can be put aside, or left on a siding, until it can be adjusted and the working of the layout as a whole will not be impaired. However, if a section of track is faulty and causes derailments it may spoil the operation of the railway entirely. It will save time and trouble in the long run if you make sure the track is properly laid at the beginning; it is always more difficult to correct faults later.

The modeller can either buy his track ready-made or he can build it himself from the component parts.

Ready-made track

The made up track now available commercially is of very good quality both in its reliability of operation and in appearance. I would recommend that the beginner should always use this type of track for his first layout. It is convenient and easy to lay and the modeller can quickly complete the basic trackwork so that it is possible to run a train. With reasonable care even a novice can lay smooth and accurate trackwork over which trains will run reliably and without derailments.

Most of the ready-made track has rail of Code 100 section in 00/HO and of Code 80 in N which represents the heaviest rail used on prototype main lines and is therefore overscale for lighter track. However, it has the great advantage of accepting virtually all proprietary wheels, whereas finer section rail will only take fine scale wheels. Provided the track is ballasted and painted (as described later) the appearance of the heavier rail is quite acceptable.

Sectional track

This is the type with which the beginner will be familiar from its inclusion in train sets. The pieces of track have the rails attached to a rigid sleeper base and are thus of fixed shape, straight or curved in a range of radii. The sections are also made in a selection of shorter lengths permitting greater scope in track arrangement. A rail joiner is fitted on one rail at each end ready for fixing the sections together.

Sectional track is the simplest and quickest to lay and can, of course, be set out temporarily and taken up again as soon as the particular track layout is finished with. If it is to be more permanent, pins can be used to hold it in place. Alternatively it can be fixed with double-sided adhesive tape. This will hold it firmly and it is still easy to lift the track again later.

The best way of joining pieces of sectional track is to lay them on a flat surface and gently slide them together so that the rails fit correctly into the joiners. This may sound obvious but it is surprisingly easy, especially with N and Z scales, to let the rail overlap the joiner instead, causing a vertical misalignment at the rail join which can lead to derailments. Similarly when taking the sections apart again slide them on a flat surface. Never twist or strain the track as this may permanently distort it. With a train set or temporary layout which is dismantled after use, the track must be stored away carefully to avoid damage. Do not just pile all the track together in a box or drawer but stack it neatly. A good idea is to wrap each section of track in tissue paper or even newspaper. The points can be kept in their original boxes if these have been retained. Be especially careful that the rail joiners do not get bent as this may interfere with smooth running and also with electrical contact. When joining the sections make sure that they are properly aligned. With the curved sections in particular it is quite easy to have a slight

Track

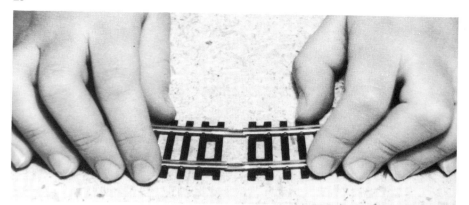

When joining pieces of sectional track place them on a flat surface and slide them together making sure the rail ends fit properly into the rail joiners. Take care not to bend or twist the track.

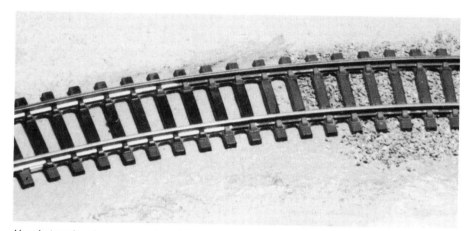

Hornby sectional track on a permanent layout. Note the great improvement in appearance of the track after ballasting and painting the rails and sleepers at the right side of the picture.

angulation at the join. One way of checking is to place another section of the same radius over the join as a guide; another is to use a Tracksetta template of the appropriate curve.

A wide range of sectional track pieces is available from various manufacturers, especially in the most popular 00/HO and N gauges. In many cases the parts from different makers are compatible which provides even greater choice. When setting up a track layout you may find that you need some small lengths of straight or curved track to complete it. Half and quarter sections, both straight and curved, are available and these may be suitable; alternatively a piece

can be cut to fit exactly, as described in the section on flexible track. Some of the manufacturers also make extendable or telescoping pieces, the lengths of which are adjustable, within limits, to fit the gap present. The points and special trackwork are suitable for use with either sectional or flexible track and are considered later.

Most sectional track consists of rails fixed to a rigid sleeper base without ballast; if this is required it must be added as with flexible track. However, the Fleischmann N-gauge 'Piccolo' track is complete with a ballast base. In 00/HO the Conrad track system, also manufactured in Germany, is a comprehensive system with a preballasted base

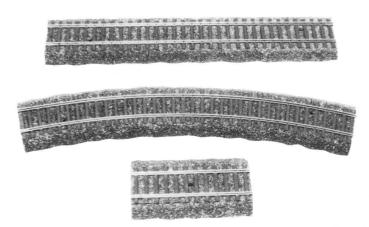

A selection of track pieces from the Conrad range of 00/HO sectional track. Note the textured and coloured ballast base moulded in plastic.

of rigid plastic. The texture and colour of the ballast is realistic and the system is designed for the enthusiast who wants to build a scale layout but wishes to have the convenience of sectional track.

Sectional track is the easiest to work with and is ideal for the beginner. It can be assembled without any cutting or other constructional work and provides a smooth running line. It can also be taken apart and rearranged as often as desired giving the modeller the chance to experiment with a variety of layout schemes. Because most modellers progress to using flexible track they often overlook the uses of the sectional variety on a permanent scale layout. It can be a very quick and convenient way of laying hidden sidings, concealed track, fiddle yards and so on; this will give reliable operation and is very desirable for any track which is hidden or inaccessible. As it is often possible to buy secondhand sectional track which is in good condition, but much cheaper than new equipment, this can be an economical way of laying such lines. There is no reason why the modeller who is going on from a train set to a permanent layout should not incorporate the sectional track he has into the new layout together with the flexible variety, and he may prefer to do this rather than scrap the former or sell it cheaply to a dealer. The sectional track is laid in the same way as flexible.

The main disadvantage of sectional track is that it is restricting. The curves are of fixed radii and this tends to result in a track plan which is rather symmetrical and toy-like. The configurations must be designed to fit the track sections available rather than the situation on the layout. However, there are many interesting and realistic plans which can be made up with this type of track.

Flexible track

On prototype railways the track is designed to fit the location and to give as smooth a ride as possible for the locomotives and rolling stock which pass over it. The track is usually laid out with smooth flowing curves and with gentle transitions from straight to curved track and this is not possible in model form using sectional track. For this reason most modellers use flexible track for their layouts.

Flexible track is similar to the usual ballastless sectional track but the plastic sleeper base, instead of being complete and rigid, has gaps arranged so that it can be curved to any desired radius. It is usually made in pieces about a yard long. To make up a layout this type of track must be curved and cut to length to fit. It must also be fixed down to keep it in position and to retain its curves.

The introduction of the modern plastic sleepered flexible track was a great advance. Prior to this the modeller either had to use sectional track with its limitations or had to make up his own trackwork, which could be very time consuming on a layout with a lot of track. The flexible track is quick and easy to lay and gives good running with a realistic appearance.

The first step is to draw out the track plan full size on the baseboard surface. It can be helpful to use points and pieces of sectional

Track

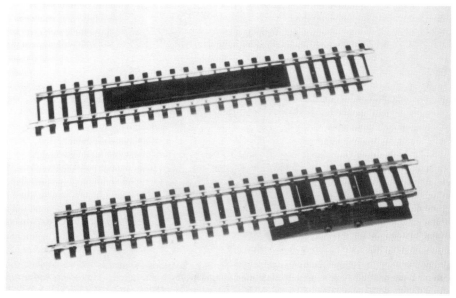

Two items of special track from the Hornby range of sectional track. Above is an uncoupling ramp fitted to a standard straight track piece; below is the isolating track section.

This 6 ft × 4 ft 00-scale layout under construction utilises track from a train set together with additional pieces of sectional track, points and flexible track. The baseboard for this layout is shown during construction in two pictures earlier in the book.

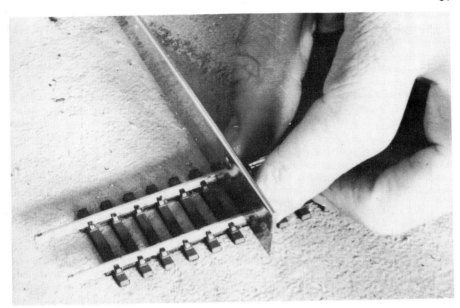

track as guides; you may also find it useful to make templates of the curves needed from hardboard, thin plywood or thick cardboard. As you set the plan out full size you may well find that you wish to make minor alterations and improvements to the layout design. Once you are satisfied with the plan, you can prepare for track laying. You will need track, points, fishplates (both insulating and non-insulating), track pins and white glue. To check each section of trackwork as it is laid you will also need a power unit, a locomotive and some rolling stock; a bogie coach and a 4-wheel wagon will suffice. This will enable you to find any faults at once so that they can be corrected before work progresses any further.

When flexible track is bent into a curve the inner rail will be too long and must be shortened to match up with the outer rail. Also the track must often be cut to fit the other track and points. This cutting is easily accomplished with a razor saw, but the rails must be held firmly while you are cutting so that you do not bend the rails or break the small tags which hold the rails to the sleepers. A small block of wood with two grooves cut in it to fit the rails forms a useful tool for holding the rails while cutting them; alternatively you can put a track gauge on to the rails close to where you cut them. After sawing through the rails use a fine file to smooth the ends, particularly the top and

To cut sectional or flexible track to fit, use a razor saw and hold the rails firmly while cutting to avoid damage to the tags which hold the rails on to the sleepers. The best method is to use a track gauge or a block of wood with two slots to fit the rails to hold the rails.

inner sides where the train wheels will run. To allow the rail joiners to slide fully by giving the proper sleeper spacing, you will need to cut along horizontally under each rail end to detach it from the first sleeper; this is easily done either with the razor saw or with a modelling knife. The filing of the rail ends mentioned above not only removes any irregularities which will interfere with smooth running but also makes it easier to slide the rail joiners on, particularly if the edges of the sides and base are slightly bevelled. If necessary the rail joiners (of the metal non-insulating type) can also be eased slightly open with the end of a screwdriver, though take care not to make them loose. Make sure that the rail joiners do not get kinked when fitting them on as this may cause misalignment at the rail joins. The joiners can be tightened after fitting using a pair of fine pliers to ensure good electrical contact. A slight gap between the rail ends will allow for any expansion and contraction with temperature changes. Where rail gaps are required for electrical isolation or sectionalisation use

Track

32

insulating rail joiners instead of the usual metal ones.

Laying ready-made track is not difficult but it should not be rushed. Take your time and make a really good job of the trackwork; it is easier to get it right to begin with than to have to try to correct it later! There are several popular methods of ballasting the track and these will be fully described a little later but I should mention at this stage that in some of these the ballast must be applied at the same time as the track is laid.

If you wish to pin the track down, and this is usually advisable at least for curved track, use the commercially available track pins. Many brands of track have holes in the sleepers at intervals for pinning. If the track you are using does not already have holes, or if you require pins in different positions, you can drill them out with a drill bit slightly larger in diameter than the pins. The pins should not be a tight fit in the holes because this may lead to the sleepers bending when the pins are pushed in. If your layout has insulation board for the baseboard top or for the track bases you can use the fine Peco track pins and with these you do not need to drill holes in the sleepers as they can be easily pushed in through the sleepers and into the insulation board. If your track is laid on a harder surface such as chipboard, plywood or blockboard stouter pins will be required and holes should be drilled both through the sleepers and into the base. The track pins are pushed in using fine long-nose pliers or a fairly strong pair of tweezers. Insert the pins with the pliers while holding the track firmly with your other hand. Push them in far enough just to touch the sleepers but do not force them in any further as this will bend the sleepers and distort the track. It is also easier to remove the pins should you wish to lift the track later to make alterations to your track plan if the pins are not too far in. On a portable layout the pinning should be fairly close to keep the track secure; on other layouts relatively few pins are required and the spacing can be wider.

The track can be glued down using white (PVA) glue. The adhesive is spread over the track area, the track is positioned and either weighted down to hold it in place or lightly pinned to prevent it moving until the glue sets. Ballast is usually applied over the glue immediately after the track is positioned. An alternative method of fixing the track down is to use double-sided adhesive tape. Pieces are cut to the lengths required and carefully fixed down in the line of the track. The protective paper covering is then peeled off and the track is laid on top. No pins are needed. Ballast is sprinkled on and pressed down with the fingers to make it adhere to the tape around the sleepers.

If a foam ballast underlay is used this should be fitted on to the sleepers before the track is laid. Adhesive can be applied to the sleepers before combining the track and underlay if you wish though this is not essential as the glue used to fix the underlay down will soak through the foam and also hold the track firm. A few pins are inserted to hold the combined track and underlay in place while the glue sets. This pinning must be done with particular care not to push the pins in too far as it is easy to compress the underlay where it is pinned producing a switchback effect with the track. The laying of points calls for especial care and details are given in the section on points and special trackwork.

It is generally best to start track laying at the most complex part of the trackwork, usually the station area. Here there may be several points and a runaround track, where the track must match up exactly. Once you have got this correct you can work along the line. In this way with an oval track plan you will be able to work round in both directions from the station and when the tracks meet you will be able to adjust the simple straight tracks to match up smoothly. If, however, you left the station area until last it might be difficult, or impossible, to get the tracks to match up accurately.

Each piece of track should be properly aligned with the preceding section. If you bring your eye down close to track level and sight along the rails you can easily see any bends or kinks and they can be corrected before the track is fixed down. When laying curves it is easy to overlook a slight kink at the join which will jolt and perhaps derail rolling stock passing over it. It is useful to cut a template from thick card, hardboard or thin plywood to the appropriate curve to fit alongside the inner side of the inner rail and the track is then curved to fit this before it is fixed down. Alternatively you can buy Tracksetta templates for the radii you will be using. These metal templates are made in a range of radii, and also straight, for 00 and N gauges and are designed to fit between the rails of the flexible track holding it to shape until it is fixed in position. With either type of template, the Tracksettas or the homemade shapes, joins can also be accurately aligned. If the curve on the layout is to be longer than the template, fix the first part of the curve down, then move the template along so half

Model Railway Guide 1

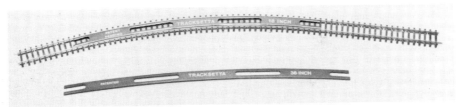

The Melcam 'Tracksetta' metal templates simplify the laying of flexible track in smooth curves and the joining of curved segments of sectional track accurately. Two N-gauge templates are shown in this picture, one of 18 in radius fitted into a length of Peco flexible track above and one of 36 in radius below. Straight templates are also produced.

is still in the fixed section of the curve while the rest curves the next part of the track into place. Continue working along the curve in stages until the whole curve is fixed down. When minimum radius curves are necessary take particular care to make them as smooth and accurate as you can so that you get good running.

It is worth while buying a track gauge even if you plan to lay only ready-made track and using it to check when track laying. Suitable gauges are made by Peco, Millholme Models and Hamblings. The most likely place for the track to get out of gauge is where two sections are joined, particularly if the joint occurs on a curve. If possible avoid having a rail joint too near to the point where a curve starts or ends. If you must have a joint here it may help to pre-bend the rails into the curve required rather than letting it take up the curve itself as you lay it. Another useful dodge when joining flexible track is to cut the track so that two or three sleepers are left beyond the ends of the rails. The rails from the next section are brought into the tags on these sleepers. This will reduce the tendency for kinking at the join.

On model railways the change from straight track to curved is usually abrupt with the track passing immediately into a curve which has the same radius throughout. This tends to cause lurching as rolling stock passes from the straight to the curve and also makes the small radius curves we have to use, due to lack of space, even more noticeable. On prototype railways this change is gradual, the track passing from straight into a curve, the radius of which steadily decreases until it reaches the radius of the curve proper. This linking curve is known as a transition or spiral curve or easement. The plotting of mathematically correct easements is complex and beyond most of us; I believe an American modeller has used a computer to calculate them for his

layout! However a very reasonable compromise can be reached by using a curve with twice the radius of the curve proper and about 8-10 in long to link the straight track with the true curve. Using this as a guide you will find that the flexible track will assume a smooth curve which is close to a true easement. To do this will, of course, need a little more space or alternatively means employing a smaller radius for the curve proper so that the curve will fit into the same space. However you will find that the running will be smoother and the appearance better with an easement even though it does mean using a sharper curve for the curve proper.

Sometimes it is necessary to fit a section of track in between two other pieces which are already fixed down, for example when completing a run-around loop or when fitting the last piece in an oval. To do this place a length of track over the gap and mark it off to the correct length. Then cut to the exact size to fit the gap. If the track piece is reasonably long, it can be sprung into place without difficulty after fitting rail joiners on to the rail ends. If the segment of track is too short for this it can still be fitted quite easily. Cut the rail joiners down to about two-thirds of their normal length and cut along under each rail end so that the shortened rail joiners can be pushed far enough back that they do not extend beyond the rail ends at all. The piece of track is then dropped into place, the rail ends lined up with those of the adjacent sections of track, and the rail joiners pushed along to fit across the joins.

On a portable layout the rails must be firmly fixed at the baseboard edge where the track crosses from one section of the baseboard to the next. The rail ends are best secured by soldering them to the heads of small screws fixed into a ½ in square edging strip of wood, if insulation board is used as the top surface, or into the chipboard if this is employed as the top.

Track

Points and special trackwork

A good selection of ready-made points and other special items of track is available, particularly in 00/HO and N gauges. These include standard points of various radii, curved points and crossings of different angles. Symmetric or Y-points save space compared to the standard points and this may be very useful in cramped situations. Two Y-points together form an arrangement similar to a double slip-point. Another space saver is the 3-way point and the rather similar lap-point; these are typically seen giving access to industrial sidings. In model form these points not only look interesting and authentic but also allow extra tracks to be fitted in. Double slip-points are expensive but well worth considering both for their impressive appearance and for the operational flexibility they introduce in a station approach, goods yard or industrial area.

I have not provided a listing of the types of points available from different manufacturers as these change with the introduction of new items and the withdrawal of others. Also from time to time a new firm begins production. When planning or constructing a model railway layout consult the current catalogues and also check with your local dealer for advice on what is available.

In many cases the points are made as both manually and electrically operated types. Some manufacturers make manually operated points to which point motors, sold as separate items, can be fitted very simply.

The points offered by some manufacturers, particularly in N scale, are designed for function rather than for authentic scale appearance. The choice is up to the individual but I would advise looking at as many different makes as possible before buying any of the points needed for your layout. The Peco 'Streamline' points and track are particularly realistic in appearance and provide smooth running as well.

Catch-points are designed to derail any stock which comes on to them when they are set against that track. They are located

An electrically operated N-gauge, left-hand, double slip-point by Fleischmann.

A Peco 00-scale, double slip-point. This impressive point will add interest to the trackwork while providing flexibility and saving space.

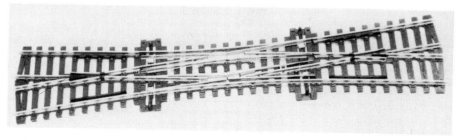

on sidings before they join main lines to make sure that stock cannot run on to the main line accidentally. They are also used on inclines to derail any wagon becoming detached from a train going up the incline. Right- and left-hand catch-points are made in N, 00 and 0 gauges by Peco.

Other special track pieces include power input sections, isolating rail sections and uncouplers. I have already mentioned the extending rail pieces made by various firms; these sections of straight track can be lengthened or shortened, within limits, to suit the gap left between two sections of track and are intended for use with sectional track. Another special item is the Fleischmann contact treadle (00/HO and N) which can be fitted on to the track and when the contact button on the underside of a Fleischmann locomotive contacts it as the engine passes over, an electrical impulse is produced which can be used to operate points, signals, and so on. A similar device is available in N scale from Arnold which is activated by the metal wheels of a passing locomotive.

Fleischmann make models of rack and pinion locomotives in HO and N scales and special track for these is produced, though no points are made. For HO scale, flexible rack rail in 8 in lengths, designed to be fitted on to ordinary straight or curved track, is available. In N-scale, flexible track is manufactured complete with a centre rack rail.

The Conrad system of sectional track, complete with moulded ballast base, was mentioned earlier. The pointwork is very interesting being based on a modular system of switches and crossings from which different types of points and crossings can be assembled. Point motors are concealed within the ballast base. There is also an uncoupling rail section.

When laying points they should be pinned down taking great care not to twist, bend or otherwise distort them; when fixed in place check that the point blades move freely. Glue

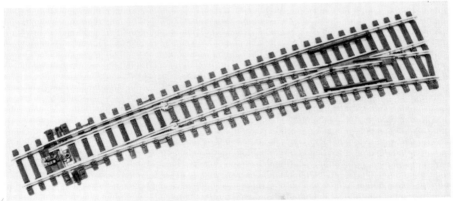

An attractive curved right-hand point in 00 scale by Peco; this is a dead frog point but the Peco 00-scale 'Streamline' points are also available with live frogs, except for crossings and double slip-points.

A Peco 0-scale, left-hand point. The 0-scale 'Streamline' points are live frog (Electrofrog) points with the frog energised through a switch built in to the toe-end of the point.

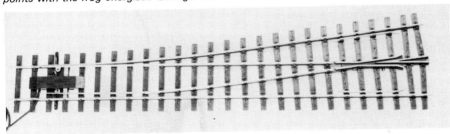

Realistic track at 'Stonepark Lane', an 00-scale branchline terminus. The track is Peco 'Streamline' with foam ballast underlay and a little additional loose ballast. Both the track and ballast have been painted to enhance the effect.

Above The Fleischmann lap-point is employed, at the left side of this picture, as the lead to these hump yard sidings on a fine Fleischmann HO-scale exhibition layout. The hump is just out of view to the left. **Below** The hump section. The whole layout including the hump yard is worked automatically using standard parts from the Fleischmann range.

may be used in addition if necessary for the ballasting though Peco recommend that glue should not be used with their points as the adhesive may adversely affect the plastic of the base. When laying standard right- or left-hand points hold a straight edge alongside the straight stock rail to make sure that the point is fixed down with this rail perfectly straight.

If foam ballast underlay is used take care not to push the pins in too far causing distortion; the heads of the pins should be just clear of the tops of the sleepers. If loose ballast glued in place is used it is essential that the ballast be kept clear of the moving parts of the point as otherwise the point may be jammed or at least have its movement impaired. Also make sure the ballast does not get between the running and check rails. When the ballast and glue have set, remove any loose ballast and check the point movement again. If necessary use a small screwdriver to scrape away any ballast which is fouling the point. Make sure that the sharp ends of the point blades rest tightly against the stock rails so that the wheel flanges will not run between; it may be necessary to file the ends of the blades very slightly to ensure this.

Point control

For points which are within easy reach of the operator simple inexpensive point levers are perfectly adequate. On a small layout, all the points may be readily accessible and these levers may be all that is needed. However, on many layouts some, at least, of the points are likely to be out of reach and some form of remote control is required. This may be electrical or mechanical.

Electrical control is generally more expensive but is very convenient, is easier to install than mechanical control and can be used to work points at any distance. It is also suitable for portable layouts as the wires can be connected at the baseboard joins to link different sections; mechanical methods could only be used to control points on the same baseboard as the control position. Many of the manufacturers offer their points as either manually or electrically operated or they make electric point motors which can simply be clipped on to the manual points to convert them. These are usually fitted on top of the baseboard surface but the Arnold (N scale) and Fleischmann (HO/00 and N scales) point motors are designed to allow mounting either on top of the baseboard or set into it, so that they can be covered and concealed. It should be noted that for the Arnold and Fleischmann motors a right-hand point motor is used inverted and set into the baseboard for a left-hand point and vice versa. The Peco point motors are designed for fitting beneath the baseboard but can be used, with an adaptor, above the baseboard. Though fixing point motors beneath or set into the baseboard gives a very good effect visually it does make access more difficult and for this reason some modellers prefer to have the motors on top of the baseboard but concealed by removable features such as a small lineside hut or a dummy, hollow stack of sleepers. The electrical details are discussed later.

A variety of mechanical methods for point control have been devised. I think the neatest and probably the easiest to install successfully is the wire-in-tube system. The points are changed by a fine wire moving within copper or plastic tubing; at one end the wire is connected to the switch blade tie bar or point lever and at the other to a lever worked by hand. A standard lever frame forms a neat arrangement for grouping together the controls for a number of points; if desired the frame can be fitted within a dummy building which is open at the rear for access to the frame.

Generally the tubing should be kept in a straight line as far as possible but curves with a radius down to 2 in can be made in it. The plastic tubing is very flexible and easy to use but must be fixed down with care so that the tubing is not constricted causing the wire to stick. When bending the more rigid copper tubing a former should be used to get a smooth curve. The tubing is relatively unobtrusive, especially if painted, and can be mounted on the baseboard surface. If the point to be controlled is beyond another track the tubing must be set into a groove to pass under the track. In fact some modellers prefer to set all the tubing into grooves so that it is concealed; the grooves are most conveniently made before the tracks are laid over them. The grooves are easy to cut if insulation board is used; they should be a good fit for the tubing to help hold it in place. Special fittings are provided to hold the plastic tubing; the copper tube can be held by, or soldered to, pins pushed into the baseboard.

Where the wire joins the point-switch blade and the lever frame, the tubing should be in a straight line with the movement of the tie bar and the lever. Bring the tube up from the groove in a gradual slope rather than at an angle. If the point control wire must turn through a right angle, an angle crank can be

Track

A Peco 00-scale left-hand catch-point. Catch-points are used on sidings and on inclines to derail rolling stock which might otherwise obstruct the main line and in model form they make an interesting and authentic detail. Peco make catch-points in N, 00, and 0 scales.

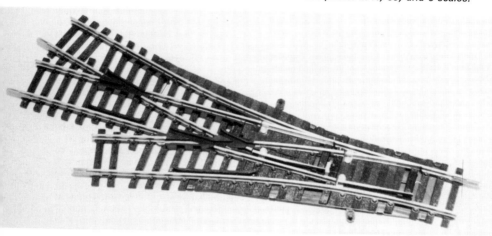

The lap-point is similar to a 3-way point but is not symmetric. It is a useful space saver in a goods yard or industrial area. The HO-scale lap-point shown here is from the Fleischmann range of points.

A diamond crossing in N gauge, by Roco. Note the insulated frogs.

used rather than bending the tubing. The point itself must be firmly fixed down so that the wire moves the tie bar and not the whole point.

The wire-in-tube method is not suitable for control over long distances. The maximum is probably about 10 ft but I prefer to limit the length to 6 ft if possible.

Constructing track

Though the introduction of flexible track has made it possible to lay very realistic track using ready-made products there are still limitations. For complete freedom in track laying giving flowing curves and pointwork to suit the particular situation, hand-built track is still the ideal if the modeller has the necessary skill and is prepared to put in the time and effort required. It also means that finer section rail than that normally used for ready-made track can be employed giving a more realistic appearance; though this will also entail the adoption of finer wheel standards for the locomotives and rolling stock.

In 0 scale Peco make sleepers, chairs which are fixed on to the sleepers with fine pins, bullhead rail and point parts enabling easy construction of well detailed track and points which match up with the ready-made items they produce.

In 00 and TT scales flat-bottom rail can be spiked down and Peco make the necessary components including 'Readiflex' sleeper bases which ensure accuracy of gauge and sleeper spacing. Alternatively flat-bottom rail can be fixed in place by gluing; this is particularly convenient in N and Z scales.

Most modellers who construct their own track in the smaller scales, 00/HO, TT and N, use soldered assembly. The rails can be soldered to pins or staples inserted into card or thin plywood sleepers, but recently the use of copper-clad sleepering has become popular for this type of construction. This material is available cut to size and ready for use with a shallow cut already made across the centre of each sleeper to insulate the two sides from one another.

Provided the modeller has some experience with soldering, construction of the track is straightforward, particularly if a jig is used. A simple jig can be made by fixing small wood strips on to a wooden base arranged so that sleepers placed between the strips will be at the correct spacing. One rail is laid alongside the ends of the strips and is soldered to the sleepers in the jig. The sleepers and single rail are moved along and

the rail is soldered to more sleepers put into the jig until the single rail has sleepers fixed along its whole length. The unit of one rail and sleepers is then laid, either straight or curved as required, and if desired ballasted. The second rail is then soldered in place using a track gauge to ensure proper positioning.

There are various methods of constructing points and the subject is rather beyond the scope of the present book. Typically the construction sequence would begin with laying the straight and curved stock rails; these are grooved to take the ends of the point blades. The frog is fitted next having carefully filed the ends of the two rail pieces which form it so that they fit accurately together. A track gauge is used to ensure correct positioning of the frog in relation to the stock rails. The point blades are shaped

A Roco N-gauge, left-hand point fitted with a point motor for electrical remote control.

An example of the wire-in-copper-tube method of control here used for an N-gauge point. The tubing will be much less conspicuous when scenic work is carried out. Alternatively the tubing can be fitted into grooves in the baseboard top surface.

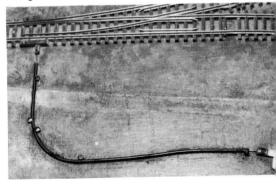

Track

Track on the 4 mm scale Swanage Branch layout constructed by the Isle of Purbeck MRC was hand-built with rail soldered to brass pins in thin-ply sleepers. Excellent overall finishing of the track and lineside area has created a very realistic appearance. Note the telegraph poles and wires, often neglected on model railways.

Points on the Swanage Branch layout were also hand-built and this picture provides a closer look at the track and points.

Two scenes on P.D. Hancock's superb 'Craig & Mertonford Railway' layout. The model is 4 mm scale 9 mm gauge and all track was hand-built. Note the unusual point at Dundreich Halt. (Both photos by P.D. Hancock.)

Superbly modelled broad-gauge track on Mike Sharman's 4 mm scale period layout. Flat-bottom Peco rail was soldered on to brass pins in sleepers of balsa. Note the authentic point levers, pointman's hut and disc signal.

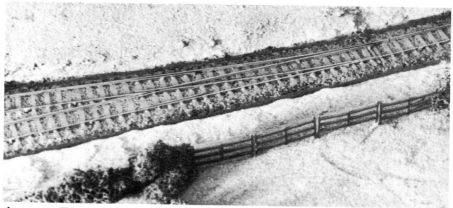

A very neat TT-scale point constructed by soldering Code 65 nickel silver rail on to copper-clad sleepers. The point is on the Great Wessex Railway layout built by John Medd.

and fitted and are fixed to the tie bar. The final pieces are the check rails.

Obviously the modeller should gain experience in the making of standard points before tackling more complex pointwork.

Narrow-gauge track
Ready-made flexible track is produced by Peco for the most popular narrow-gauges, 009 (4 mm scale 9 mm gauge) and 016.5 (7 mm scale 16.5 mm gauge) and this firm also makes points, standard right- and left-hand, for 009. It is also possible to use the ordinary track and points made for the gauge in question even though they are intended for standard gauge in a smaller scale. The

sleeper size and spacing will not be correct but if the track is well ballasted and the sleepers are largely hidden this is not obvious and the appearance can be perfectly satisfactory. This method does give the convenience of a much wider range of track and points.

Of course the modeller can scratchbuild his own track and points using the components available for standard-gauge track and employing the same methods.

Dual-gauge track
Modelling narrow-gauge prototypes introduces the possibility of including some dual-, or even triple-gauge track on a layout. Such trackwork can be complex and a great many

A scene on Howard Coulson's very attractive 4 mm scale 9 mm gauge layout based on East African narrow-gauge prototypes. Howard used standard N-scale track to represent 00-scale narrow gauge and the effect is very good even though strictly the sleeper sizes and spacing are not correct, as the track is well ballasted.

Two 009 narrow-gauge points of soldered construction built by Terry Jenkins for a quarry line. The method is similar to that for standard-gauge pointwork.

varied arrangements for points are possible. Though a few ready-made dual-gauge track items have been commercially produced such special trackwork will generally have to be built by hand. Methods are essentially similar to those used for ordinary track but there are more parts to be fitted. The modeller would be well advised to gain some experience of building single-gauge track and points before tackling dual-gauge. It is also best to study the prototype arrangements and to choose one of the simpler examples for a first attempt.

Ballasting

Unless you are using track already complete with a ballast base, such as the Conrad range, the track you lay, whether it is ready-made or hand-built, must be ballasted to give a realistic appearance.

There are various methods of ballasting, most of which must be carried out at the time the track is laid. An easy and convenient method is to use foam plastic underlay. The foam has a cushioning effect which helps to produce quiet, smooth running. The only disadvantages are the greater cost and the fact that it has a slightly less realistic appearance than loose ballast. However, with painting and a sprinkling of loose ballast applied over glue the appearance of the foam underlay can be very good indeed. (The method of laying track with foam underlay was described earlier.) Do not use an

This page Brian Harrap has three gauges on his 1:87 scale (HO) layout, 8.7 mm, 11.5 mm and 16.5 mm and his trackwork includes dual- and even triple-gauge track. (All photos by Brian Harrap.) **Top** A simple diversion of the 8.7mm gauge from the 11.5 mm gauge with only one acute and one obtuse angle crossing. As this is a freight-only turnout no moving blades have been fitted. **Centre** Here a left-hand narrow-gauge point is superimposed on a right-hand standard-gauge point producing four frogs and four blades, two of which overlap. **Below** More complex dual-gauge track at the entrance to the goods yard and the 8.7 mm gauge and 11.5 mm gauge passenger platforms.

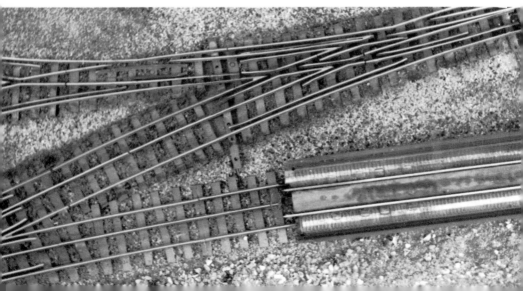

excessive amount of adhesive as this will soak through the foam and when it hardens will make the underlay stiff, thus reducing its cushioning effect.

If you wish to use loose ballast, usually cork granules appropriately coloured, or fine granite chippings, it is best applied when the track is laid as it is almost impossible to paint glue neatly around the sleepers for later ballasting without getting it on to the sleepers or rails. The track area is marked out and a covering of latex adhesive is applied. The track is then laid in position and pinned down. Ballast is sprinkled on covering the whole area and is pressed down into the glue. The whole thing is then left to set until completely dry after which excess ballast can be brushed off for re-use elsewhere. Any bare patches are touched up with a little glue and extra ballast. As I mentioned earlier it is essential to make sure that no adhesive is applied to the base where the moving parts of points will be and that no glue gets on to these parts. Failure to take sufficient care here may spoil the smooth working of the points; particularly important if the points are to be controlled electrically as the motors may be unable to overcome any increased resistance to movement. Peco points should not be glued down and with these the glue must be applied around the sleepers after laying for ballasting, again taking care not to get any glue on the moving parts.

An excellent method of ballasting devised in the United States is the so-called 'bonded ballast' technique. Loose ballast is applied dry to the track after laying and is spread out around and between the sleepers using a small brush. The ballast is kept clear of the moving parts of points. Once you are satisfied with the appearance of the ballast it can be sprayed with water containing a few drops of detergent such as washing up liquid, using a perfume spray, atomiser or airbrush. This spraying must be gentle so that the ballast is not displaced; the idea is to apply a mist of water, just enough to dampen the ballast. Then drops of a solution of 1 part of acrylic matte medium (available from art shops) to 6 parts of water are applied using an eyedropper. The drops spread easily through the ballast due to the previous damping with the detergent solution. When the process is completed leave to dry overnight. Then gently brush off any loose ballast and do any touching up needed. Remove any adhesive or ballast which has stuck to the running surfaces of the rails.

As an alternative to the acrylic matte medium, diluted white glue can be used.

However the glue dries hard whereas the matte medium remains more flexible and resilient giving a cushioning effect.

Track detailing

For the most realistic appearance the track requires further detailing. Before starting on this I would suggest that you go and have a good look at the real thing. Usually we spend our time watching the trains or looking at the buildings rather than the track but just a few minutes study will make you much more aware of the colours of the rails, sleepers and ballast, and of the many small details always present on and near the tracks.

The most important single aspect is the colouring. Real rails are either dark brown or rust colour on all surfaces except those on which the train wheels run. Painting the rails of the track on your layout with rust colour (Humbrol include 'Rust' in their range of paints) and wiping off the top surfaces before the paint dries will give a great improvement in appearances. It will also do much to conceal the fact that the rail used in ready-made track is overscale. You may also like to paint the sleepers with dark brown paint (Humbrol 'Track Colour' is suitable) to give them a more weathered appearance. The colour of the ballast can be toned down with a light overspray of brown in an airbrush if you want to make it look less clean and new. An easy method of representing old track and ballast is to spray the whole thing with track colour, wiping the tops of the rails clean and touching up the sides of the rails with rust colour. In areas where coal dust and oil drop onto the track the ballast will be discoloured and this can be simulated with black paint.

Buffer stops are available ready-made and in kit form for both sleeper and rail built types; these should also be carefully painted and weathered. Dummy point levers are made by Peco and by Dart Castings and are a nice detail touch even if the points are actually operated electrically by concealed motors. Colin Waite has introduced a kit of parts for accurate modelling of the point rodding used on prototype railways to control many points. Assembly is rather time consuming and requires care but the results are very realistic and greatly enhance the appearance of the track.

There are many other small items which can easily be added; ATC (Automatic Train Control) ramps between the rails, spare rails and track parts beside the track, speed restriction signs and warning notices, mileposts, gradient posts and so on.

Track

In dock and industrial areas tracks are often inset and this can be effectively represented in model form. The 00-scale track shown here was modelled by fixing extra rails on to Peco track leaving a sufficient gap for the wheels. Polyfilla was then used to fill the space between these inner rails and was also brought up the outer sides of the running rails. After the filler had set, a scriber was used to mark out the setts. The final step was painting.

The scratch-built point levers add the finishing touch to the track on Jim Gadd's 009 layout. Note also the pile of sleepers, a typical lineside feature.

An attractive scene on a 4 mm scale diorama by John Piper (Accessories) Limited showing the use of many of their scenic modelling products. Note the realistically ballasted track and the neat lineside fencing of various types.

Trackside details on Keith Gowen's TT-scale layout include token exchange apparatus (just in front of the goods shed). Note also the railwaymen's track crossing simply modelled from scraps of wood.

Two views of the late Eric Kay's Sherrington Branch. Note how good ballasting has given a very realistic appearance to the proprietary track. The effect has also been enhanced by the painting of the rails with rust-coloured matt enamel.

Track cleaning

Any dirt on the track will interfere with the electrical pick-up by the locomotives. For smooth running on a layout it is essential that the track is kept clean. One method of cleaning is to rub over the running surfaces of the rails with an abrasive cleaner such as the type made by Peco. This is like a hard rubber eraser. Never use sandpaper to clean the track as this will scratch the rails; dirt then collects quickly in the scratches causing further problems.

Alternatively one of the solvent cleaners can be applied to the track, either with a small piece of rag held in the hand or with one of the special track cleaning wagons produced by various manufacturers. Several cleaners marketed specifically for track cleaning are available or you can use one of the electrical cleaning fluids. If you use an abrasive cleaner this produces loose dirt and it is advisable to wipe the rails afterwards with one of the electrical cleaners.

A completely different approach to the problem is the use of a high frequency generator unit as described later.

Track

Electrification

Much of the fascination of model railways lies in the fact that they can duplicate in miniature virtually all aspects of prototype railway operation. The use of electricity to power the models has made such realistic control possible. Almost all model railways nowadays are run on 12 volts DC and utilise 2-rail electrification and I propose to discuss only this system in this book.

In their efforts to create even greater realism many expert modellers have devised complex and sophisticated control schemes. Such projects often benefit us all directly or indirectly because they lead to improvements and advances in the equipment produced commercially and hence to better control for our layouts. However, they may lead the beginner to believe that model railway electrification must always be complicated and difficult. This is not so; the electrification of a simple layout of the type a beginner is likely to be constructing is quite straightforward if a few simple rules are followed.

The basic circuit

The basic 2-rail model railway circuit consists of a power source, leads to one rail and from the other, the two rails themselves and the locomotive linking the rails. So that the current flowing through the circuit cannot be short-circuited, bypassing the motor of the locomotive, the two rails must be insulated from each other and similarly the wheels on the two sides of the engine must be insulated. The current passes from one rail to the wheels on that side of the locomotive where one or more pick-ups make contact and carry the current to the motor. The circuit is completed by the pick-ups and wheels on the other side of the engine. The current causes the motor to turn and the locomotive to move. Reversing the current direction results in the motor turning the opposite way and the locomotive moving in the opposite direction.

Though the motors used in model locomotives are rated at 12 volts DC they

usually operate at less, working at between 4 and 12 volts depending on the speed; the greater the voltage applied, the faster the engine will run. The current drawn will vary for different locomotives but for any one depends on the load (number of coaches or wagons hauled, steepness of a gradient, etc).

To control the speed and direction of travel of a locomotive a variable source of power is required and this is an opportune time to consider the types of power units available.

Power units

Train sets generally include only a battery controller; this is adequate at first but control is limited and the regular replacement of the batteries becomes expensive. As you develop your train set into a more elaborate system or into a permanent layout you will want to change to a unit working from the mains supply.

Mains power units usually have a transformer, to reduce the mains voltage of 240 to 12, a rectifier, to convert the AC (Alternating Current) to DC (Direct Current) and a controller for speed and direction, mounted together inside a single unit. It is important to remember that although the output from such a unit is perfectly safe the input is the potentially dangerous mains voltage and under no circumstances should the unit be opened up; if there is a fault take the power unit to a dealer or return it to the makers.

While I do not want to confuse the issue with unnecessary details, there are a few general points which will help you to decide which of the three main types of unit to choose. Each type has a transformer and a rectifier but the method of control employed differs.

In the simplest type, the variable resistance controller, a variable resistance is placed in series in the 12 volt DC output from the transformer and rectifier. This resistance takes part of the voltage, wasting it in the form of heat, leaving the remainder for the locomotive motor. If most of the resistance is included in the circuit relatively little voltage is available for the motor and the locomotive moves slowly. As the control is moved to leave less and less of the resistance in the circuit the engine moves faster. This system is cheap and works adequately but there are disadvantages. A basic defect is that it does not directly control the voltage to the locomotive. The track voltage depends not only on the resistance of the controller but also on the ratio between the resistances of the motor and the controller. Thus different motors need varied settings on the controller for the same voltage and ideally the resistance of the controller should be matched to the locomotive motor. The voltage wasted in the variable resistance also depends on the load and unfortunately it increases with an increase in load. Thus on a layout with gradients, instead of maintaining a uniform speed the train will slow down going uphill and speed up going down. For various reasons, including pole locking and mechanical friction, slightly more voltage is required to start the motor turning than to keep it turning slowly once it has started. This means that as the voltage increases the locomotive suddenly moves off at speed; not at all a realistic representation of the gradual start of a real train! With a variable resistance controller this is aggravated because as the locomotive starts to move the load drops and causes a rise in voltage making the engine move even faster.

The addition of a pulse power facility will help to give slower, smoother, more realistic starts. Normally full wave rectification is used so that both phases of the AC cycle are utilised; by changing to half wave using only one phase of each cycle a series of pulses are delivered to the motor with 60 pulses each second. These pulses nudge the motor into rotating without supplying enough steady voltage to send the train racing off. This results in smooth starts, good slow running and pulling power but does cause motors to become hotter than on full wave rectified DC. A power unit with pulse power is usually arranged so that half or full wave can be selected merely by moving a switch. Thus half wave can be used to start the train, with a change to full wave for running it if desired.

The variable transformer type of controller overcomes the basic failing of the variable resistance type. Here the voltage is directly controlled and the voltage selected determines the speed of the motor. Variations in load do not affect the speed as the extra load is automatically provided by the transformer. The voltage required is produced by the primary unit and this is supplied to the track; there is no need for voltage to be wasted as heat, and so less heat is produced. Pulse power can be provided on units of this type as with the variable resistance controllers.

The most recently developed type is the transistor controller. These are very efficient and produce an almost constant output regardless of varying load, and hence current. In units of this type very sophisticated control can be provided by electronic means. These include representation of the inertia and weight of the prototype with slow starting and stopping, coasting and braking. Transistor controllers can give very realistic operation even with simple proprietary locomotive models.

On power units of all types the control of speed and direction may be by a knob or lever. In some cases there is a centre 'off' position with forward one side and reverse the other. In others there is a separate reversing switch and the whole range of

This Airfix unit is typical of the battery controllers supplied with train sets.

The H & M (Hammant & Morgan) 'Safety Minor' is a variable transformer power unit with pulse power and is an ideal unit for a beginner. In addition to the controlled DC output there are uncontrolled 16 volt AC and 12 volt DC auxiliary outputs.

The Digitol 'Gemini T', by Southern Electronic Consultants, is an electronic controller with excellent control, including automatic load compensation, inertia and weight simulation and smooth stopping and starting.

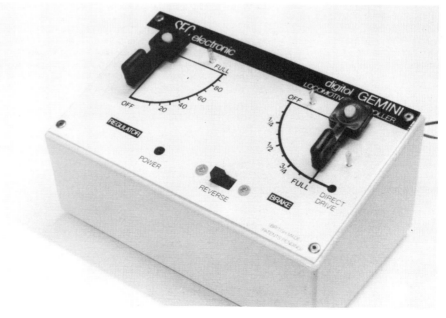

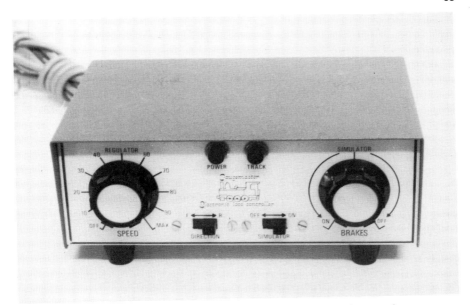

The 'Gaugemaster' is another electronic controller giving realistic operation.

movement of the knob or lever is used to control speed.

Many power units have, in addition to the controlled 12 volt DC output to the track, an auxiliary 16 volt AC uncontrolled outlet for working point motors and other accessories.

Basic wiring

To run a locomotive on a section of track all we need do is connect wires from the controlled DC output terminals of the power unit to the rails. There are terminal rail sections and clips of various types designed for fixing these wires to the rails for sectional track. These can be used on a permanent scale layout but the best method is to solder the wires to the sides of the rails. Suitable wire is available from model railway dealers and electrical shops.

This is all that is required for a length of track, a basic oval, or even for a simple layout, provided dead frog points are employed and we wish to run only one locomotive.

In considering the wiring of a layout we must distinguish carefully between the different types of points available, and here I am referring to the electrical differences not to those in the geometric pattern. The essential feature is whether the frog is electrically live or not as this affects the wiring required.

Dead frog points

In these the frog is made from plastic and is electrically dead. This type of point is very simple to wire but has the disadvantage that locomotives may stall or falter as they pass over the non-electrified frog. Dead frog points can themselves be divided into two types, non-isolating and self-isolating. In the former type the rails beyond the frog are wired so that all the rails are live whichever way the point is set. This makes wiring a layout extremely simple; the current can be fed in at any point and the whole layout will be live at all times. This is, however, at the expense of the convenience of using points for isolation.

In the self-isolating type the point blade is wired to the rail, beyond the frog, on to which it leads, but not to the stock rail. The point blades have a contact so that the one which touches the stock rail is live while the other is isolated. This means that a siding from a self-isolating point is live when the point is set for it but dead when the point is set against it. Unlike a layout with non-isolating points the whole layout is not live and the feed point must be suitably positioned.

The rule for wiring dead frog points is that the current must be fed to the toe-end of a point. This does not mean that a separate feed is needed for each point as a series of

Electrification

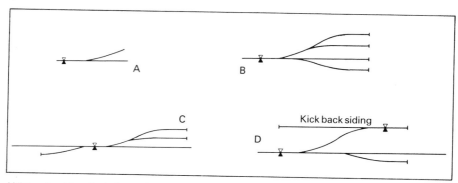

Wiring dead frog isolating points. A Feed must always be at the toe-end of a point. B Only one feed is needed for a series of points all facing the same way. C One feed will supply points at either side provided the feed is at the toe-ends of the points. D For a kickback siding another feed at the toe-end of the point leading to it is required. Dead frog points require gaps only for isolating purposes.

points facing the same way can all be supplied by one feed at the toe-end of the first point. If a kick-back siding is included a further feed will be needed at the toe-end of this point as shown in the diagram.

The wiring of a small layout with dead frog points of either type is very simple and I would recommend that the beginner use points of the dead frog variety. Any pick-up problems causing locomotive stalling on the dead frogs can usually be overcome by making sure that the wheel treads and current collectors are kept clean. It is also important that there is pick-up from at least two pairs of wheels and preferably more; on tender engines collectors can also be fitted to pick up from the tender wheels with advantage.

Live frog points
In this type of point the frog is metal and is electrically live ensuring good pick-up as a locomotive crosses over it. The frog is wired to the point blades to that both blades and the frog have the same polarity as the stock rail with which the blade is in contact. In this way the track for which the point is set has rails of opposite polarity. The rails of the track against which the point is set have the same polarity and therefore no current will flow; this is because they are electrically linked at this setting.

There are two rules for the electrification of live frog points. As with the dead frog isolating type, current must be fed in at the toe-end of the point. Because there would be a short-circuit if current were fed directly to the frog in this type of point there is also another requirement. Where a feed does lead

directly to a point frog there must be an electrical gap in both rails of the track. This applies to an oval, in which there must be gaps in both rails between the feed and the frog of a point leading to a siding, and whenever two points are arranged so that the frogs face each other, as in a crossover or passing loop. Diamond crossings and slip-points are complicated to wire for live frogs and I would advise the use of dead frog crossings and slip-points even if live frog standard points are employed on a layout.

Sectionalisation
So far we have been concerned with using only one locomotive on a layout. Once we add further engines we must arrange the electrification of the layout so that we can control each locomotive. To do this we divide the system up into sections, each of which can be switched on or off as we wish. Provided we only intend to move one locomotive at any one time the single controller is all that is required; it is connected to all the sections but only those in use are switched on. Any locomotive on a section which is switched off will not move.

A simple form of section is the isolated section on a dead-end track, for example an engine shed siding. One rail is gapped by cutting through it with a razor saw and inserting an insulating rail joiner. The rails at either side of the gap are linked by a wire with an on/off switch. If you do not want to make this arrangement up you can use one of the isolating track units designed for use with sectional track instead. In this case the track section would be included during construction or, if you decide to fit it later, a section of

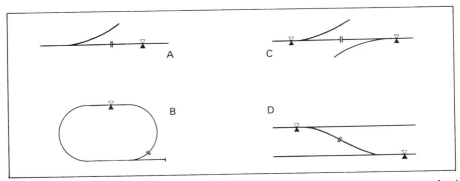

Above *Wiring live frog points.* **A** *Feed must be at the toe-end of the point; wherever a feed leads directly to a point, the frog must have insulating gaps in both rails.* **B** *In an oval with a siding there must be gaps in both rails between the feed and the frog.* **C** *Wherever the frogs of two points face each other there must be gaps in both rails.* **D** *Similarly on a crossover the point frogs face each other and both rails must have gaps.*

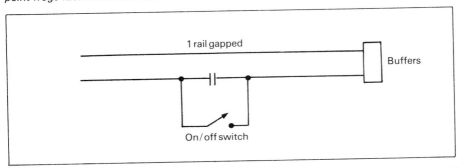

Above *Isolating Section. One rail only is gapped and this is bridged by a wire with an on/off switch. When the section is switched on it receives power from the adjacent live section.* **Below** *Sectionalisation. Full sections are, unlike the simple isolating section, completely independent with both rails gapped and with their own feeds. Return can be grouped into a common return. Each section has its own on/off switch; in the diagram, sections 2 & 3 are 'on', section 1 is 'off'.*

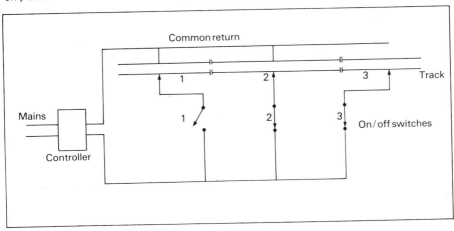

Electrification

track would be removed to allow the unit to be fitted. When switched on the isolated section receives current from the live section next to it; when switched off the section is dead and a locomotive stored here will not move when another engine is run elsewhere on the layout.

With dead frog isolating points there is a similar effect but with the switching carried out by the points instead of by on/off switches. A siding is isolated if the point is set against it and a passing loop will be isolated if the points at the ends are both set against it.

On a small layout sectionalisation of this type may be perfectly adequate and has the advantage of being very simple to arrange. However, greater flexibility of operation will be achieved by more extensive sectionalisation using independent sections each of which is completely isolated from the others and has separate current feed and return with an on/off switch.

The arrangement of the sections depends not only on the particular layout plan but also on the way in which you will operate the system so no precise instructions can be given. There are, however, some general principles which can be applied. The rules given for wiring live frog points also form a useful basis for sectionalisation whether you are using live or dead frog points. Working from your layout plan look for places where tracks lead off in one or both directions and site feeds here at the toe-ends of the points. For a series of points all facing the same way a feed at the toe-end of the first point will serve them all. Gaps in both rails are required wherever the frogs of two points face each other or the frog of a point is directly connected to a feed.

In meeting these requirements the gaps can often be placed anywhere along the length of track. To decide on the best positions think about train movements on the railway and place the gaps where they will be most convenient for the planned operational pattern.

In addition wherever trains are run on the layout there must be at least one pair of gaps between any two trains. After locating the gaps and feeds as above it may well be that some of the sections are very long. Dividing these into two or more separate smaller sections may provide more flexibility in operation. I have already mentioned isolated sections for dead-end tracks and these can be added as desired to the layout.

The system described above permits us to have two or more locomotives on the layout and to control whichever of these we wish, using a single power unit, provided that we are content to run only one engine at any one time. As a layout develops and becomes more extensive and as additional locomotives are acquired the modeller may wish to run two trains simultaneously on the railway.

Running two trains

Apart from the electrical requirements the layout must obviously be sufficiently extensive to accommodate two trains in action at the same time. Two separate power units are needed for control and the layout should be divided up into sections as described above.

The simplest method is to bring the sections together into two groups each controlled by one power unit. Two trains can be operated simultaneously on the layout provided one is in each group of sections. However, if the trains are in different sections in the same group only one can be in action the other being isolated in a switched off section. Thus, there are limitations to this simple system. Another problem arises in the transfer of a train from a section controlled by one power unit into an adjacent section under the control of the other unit. To do this the two controllers are adjusted to approximately the same setting and the train runs across from one section to the other.

An alternative arrangement to this is the provision of a section between the two groups which can be connected to either controller. In operation a train is run from one group of sections into this common section and stopped at a station. Control of this section is then switched to the other controller and the train is restarted and run on into the other group.

However, the system still has limited scope and a much better arrangement is the method known as cab control in which all sections are common to both controllers.

Simple cab control

In this system the operator takes over a cab and by switching on the sections on which he wishes to run his train he can take it anywhere on the layout except on to sections already in use for another train. There are various forms of cab control depending on the size of the layout and its complexity, on how many operators and trains there will be, and on whether the system will be worked from one central point or from a number of different positions.

For a small to moderate sized home layout on which two trains will be run by one or two operators from a central control panel, a cab control system can be simply and easily set up. Two separate power units are used, so that common return wiring can be employed, and these are placed one at either side of the control panel. On this central panel are mounted a series of single-pole double-throw centre 'off' position switches, one for each section of the layout. These switches are wired uniformly so that the same end of each is linked to one controller, and the other to the second controller. If the switches are mounted so that the lever movement is from side to side, instead of the more usual up and down, the wiring can be arranged so that the controller towards which a lever points will be the one to which the section is linked at the time. The levers can be mounted in the appropriate positions on a diagrammatic panel, on which the layout plan is drawn out in schematic form, making a very neat panel which is easy to work. Alternatively the switches can be arranged in one or more ranks, labelled to match up with a separate track plan.

Once an operator has finished using a section he should switch it to the centre 'off' position on the panel so that it is available for the other operator to use. With this particular system a section can only be linked to one controller at one time because of the switching method used.

The cab control system is an excellent one and in its simple form, as described here, is certainly not beyond the scope of the beginner once he has become familiar with the basic principles of model railway electrification.

Reversing loops

When the diverging tracks from a point are joined up to form a reversing loop, so called because the direction of travel of a train passing round the loop will have been reversed when it passes back on to the main track, an electrical problem arises. If we follow one of the rails around the loop we find that it meets the other rail at some point resulting in a permanent short-circuit. To prevent this the loop is made in a separate section isolated from the remainder of the layout by gaps in both rails at both ends of the loop.

The loop can be powered in several different ways. A simple method, which also has the advantage of allowing trains to pass round the loop without stopping, is to wire the loop directly to the controller while the leads to the main line go via a DPDT (Double-Pole Double-Throw) switch.

As the train passes on to the loop section the point is changed and the DPDT switch is thrown reversing the current in the main line; this then matches the polarity of the far end of the loop and the train can pass back on to the main line without stopping. As the feed

Simple Cab Control. Each section is linked to both controllers so either operator can use it. Each section has its own single-pole, double-throw (SPDT) switch with centre 'off' position; thus a section can be linked to one or other controller or to the 'off' position. In the diagram, section 1 is linked to controller A, section 3 to controller B and section 2 is switched off.

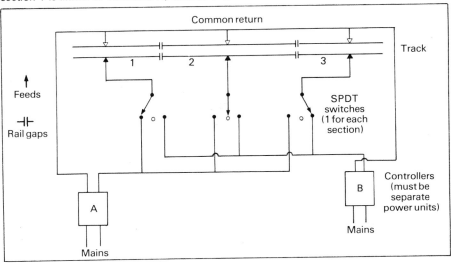

Electrification

58

reversal in the main line has been carried out by the reversing switch the direction of travel of the locomotive still matches that selected on the controller.

The reversing loop of this type is easy to identify but in designing layouts, particularly complicated ones, reversing sections can sometimes be incorporated unintentionally and without the modeller realising that they are present. An example is in the so-called dog bone or dumbell type of track plan in which the two sides of a long oval are brought together and resemble true double track. The modeller may then be tempted to introduce a crossover between these tracks. In fact the tracks are not true double track but two single tracks in opposite directions and a train passing over a crossover here will have its direction around the layout reversed. In other words a reversing section has been created. One way of checking for hidden reversing sections on a layout plan is to draw arrows in one direction along the main route. Then follow along in this direction over the

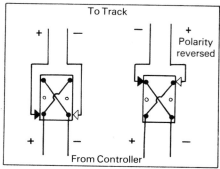

Details of DPDT switch showing how it reverses polarity when its position is changed. Centre position is 'off'.

possible routes and if at any time you find that, without stopping and reversing, you are travelling against the arrows then you have traversed a reversing section. This must either be eliminated or suitably wired. In general I would advise the beginner to avoid

Reversing loop wiring. Wiring arrangement shown permits the train to run round loop and back on to the main line without stopping. Once the train is on the loop section, which is completely isolated by gaps in both rails at both ends of the loop, the DPDT (Double-Pole Double-Throw) switch is changed, reversing polarity on main-line.

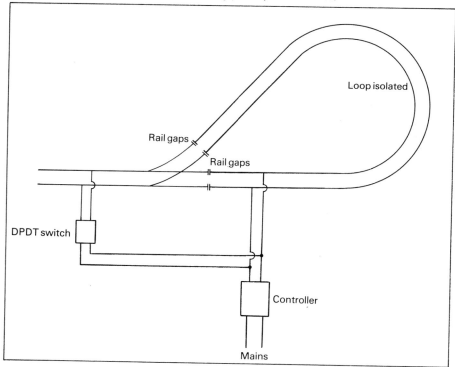

Vollmer N-scale catenary on a German prototype layout. The locomotive is a Fleischmann track cleaning engine.

Highly detailed working catenary system constructed from Sommerfeldt parts on a Fleischmann HO-scale exhibition layout.

including any reversing sections on his layout.

Catenary

A good selection of electric outline locomotive models is available in HO and N scales, mainly of American and Continental prototypes and many of these have working pantographs which can be used as the electrical pick-ups for power and control of the models. The provision of a working catenary not only adds to the realism but also provides the opportunity to control two locomotives independently and simultaneously on the same stretch of track, one being powered from the track and the other from the overhead. The simplest and cheapest working catenary was manufactured by Triang but this is no longer produced and is difficult to obtain secondhand. Two Continental firms, Vollmer and Sommerfeldt, produce parts for constructing working catenary in HO and N scales. The Sommerfeldt parts, available in Britain from M & R (Model Railways) Ltd., are highly detailed replicas of various European prototype catenary parts and are very realistic; however, it would be expensive to install more than a very limited system. Excellent working catenary systems in 00/HO scale are now also available from Lima and Hadley/J.V. The Arnold N-scale catenary is a dummy non-working system intended for appearance only. Some modellers have constructed successful catenary from scratch but this does involve a good deal of work on any but a very small layout.

Electric point control

Electric point control is very convenient to install and operate and can be used to change points at any distance. Normally twin-solenoid motors are employed in which two opposing coils move an iron core, linked to the point tie bar, changing the points. There must also be a device to lock the point after it has been thrown. The motors take a high current but for only a very short time so any number of points can be operated from a single power unit provided they are changed one at a time and not simultaneously. Many control units provide a suitable auxiliary low voltage AC output for this purpose. Using the train controller to power point motors can sometimes lead to momentary slowing of the train as points are changed so you may prefer to use a separate transformer for point control.

The impulse must be only momentary or the coil may burn out so special passing

contact, or flash, switches are employed. As with the cab control section switches mentioned earlier these can be fitted at the appropriate positions on a diagrammatic control panel. Alternatively they can be mounted in a bank or banks and numbered or otherwise coded for identification. Various firms produce suitable switches; H & M produce a neat unit containing six switches.

Some point motors, for example the H & M SW3, have an automatic cut-off switch incorporated in them so that they can be used with ordinary on/off switches instead of requiring flash switches.

An alternative method of switching points is to use two pushbuttons for each motor. However, this system does not give a visible indication on the control panel of which way the point is switched. Another popular scheme in conjunction with a diagrammatic track layout control panel is the use of an electric pencil probe, such as those made by ECM and Peco, for point changing. Two small roundheaded brass screws are inserted into the panel, one at either side of the point. Where the screws protrude through the rear of the panel, wires are attached and led to the point motor. The wiring is arranged so that the point movements match the screw positions. The electric probe is attached to the AC outlet lead. To change a point the probe is touched on the appropriate screw.

The pushbutton and electric pencil methods have the advantage that they can be kept in contact until the point is thrown whereas flash switches may not always change the point. The addition of a capacitor discharge unit will eliminate the danger of point motors burning out and also doubles the energy for operation overcoming sticking. The ECM unit, for example, is easily inserted into existing systems and can be fed from the normal 16 volt AC auxiliary supply. One unit only is required for the whole layout. The Codar 'Track King' electronic controller includes built in switching for 6-point motors and a capacitor discharge power supply output for use with any number of point motors.

Recent developments

I mentioned at the beginning of the section on electrification that expert modellers with a special interest in electrification and electronics had made many advances in the development of systems and devices giving better and more realistic operation. Fortunately the great popularity of railway modelling makes it worthwhile for manufacturers to produce many of these commercially, to the benefit of us all. I would like to conclude by mentioning three recent developments of interest.

Multiple train control

It has long been the ambition of the keen operator to be able to control several locomotives independently on the same tracks, just as on the prototype. The old Trix Twin system permitted two engines to be operated together under individual control but this required the use of 3-rail track. The centre rail was common and the other two rails each supplied one of the engines. A similar form of control is possible using working catenary with one locomotive controlled from the overhead wire and the other from the track.

However, these are special cases and in addition allow control of only two engines. The ideal is independent running of several locomotives on 2-rail track and without the need for the complication of sectional cab control. Some advanced modellers have devised various ways of achieving this including radio control and complex electronic systems but these have been beyond the ability of the average modeller.

Now multiple train control systems are being developed commercially in this country. Two major manufacturers, Airfix and Hornby, and two firms specialising in electrical equipment for model railways, H & M and ECM, are producing systems which should be on the market during the next year or so. Full technical details are not being released by any of the firms but the four systems are probably similar in principle though it seems likely that none will be compatible with any of the others.

The Airfix system, which will probably be the first to appear in the shops, permits the simultaneous independent control of four locomotives and up to 16 locomotives can be on the same track without the need for any isolating switches. This is achieved with only two wires to the track. The track is powered with 20 volts AC with each train selecting part of the current to operate only when commanded by the console. Each locomotive has a small easily fitted electronic chip inside which is set to respond only to its own signals from the control panel. The constant track power at 20 volts AC allows full coach lighting even when the train is stationary. The system will also be able to control other parts of the layout such as points and signals.

Though it will obviously take time to assess the various systems once they appear it does seem certain that electronic multiple train

The Peco point motor fits beneath the baseboard or, with an adaptor, on top of the baseboard. The motor does not have a locking device as it is designed for use with Peco points which themselves incorporate a locking spring.

Below A Hammant & Morgan point motor mounted on top of the baseboard for convenient access. **Bottom** The motor is concealed by this small hut made from Superquick kit parts.

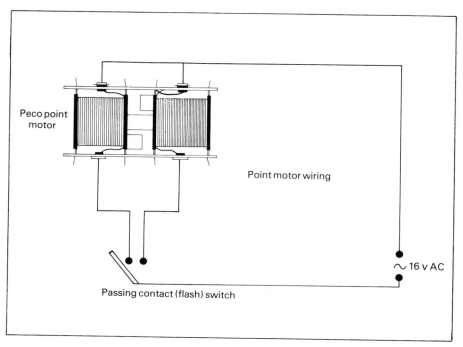

Peco point
motor

Point motor wiring

∿ 16 v AC

Passing contact (flash) switch

Point Motor Wiring. **Above** *Passing contact or flash switch.* **Below** *Electric pencil probe.*

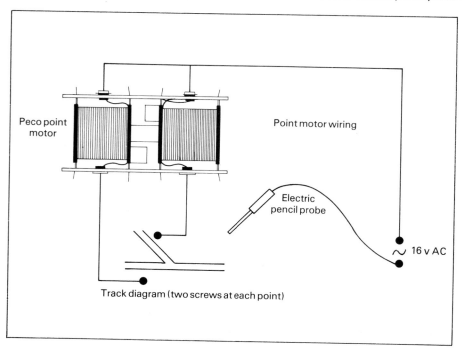

Peco point
motor

Point motor wiring

Electric
pencil probe

∿ 16 v AC

Track diagram (two screws at each point)

The control panel on Vernon Sparrow's 00-scale layout. Note the electric pencil probe just to the left of the centre of the controls and the roundheaded screws, two per point, fixed into the adjacent track diagram and used to make contact for changing the points. (Photo by Vernon Sparrow.)

The console for the Airfix Multiple Train Control system with the four control units for independent running of four locomotives. (Photo courtesy of Airfix.)

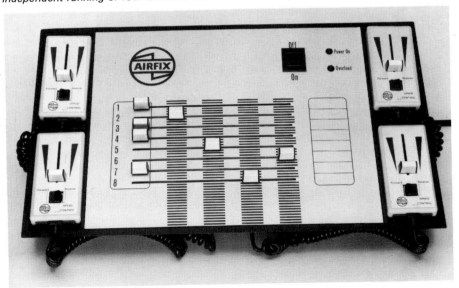

Electrification

control will revolutionise model railway electrification, perhaps making much of what I have written in this book obsolete and of historic interest only!

Sound

Another electronic development which has become popular, particularly in the United States, is the production of simulated steam and diesel locomotive sounds synchronised with the movements of the model engines. Many enthusiasts find that such a unit adds greatly to the effect and realism of operating their locomotives and gives them much enjoyment. No tapes or recordings are necessary, the sounds being synthesised electronically. The Codar 'Steamsound' unit realistically simulates all the sounds of a real steam locomotive including the exhaust beat (variable in speed and character), steam hiss, safety valve blast, the whistle (variable in pitch for different engines), and other effects!

Electric track cleaning

One of the problems in ensuring good and reliable operation is the need for the track to be kept clean so that electrical conduction is maintained. An alternative to the physical cleaning methods described in the section on

The Relco HF Generator for track cleaning.

track is the use of a high frequency generator. The Relco HF Generator, which had the distinction of being demonstrated on the 'Tomorrow's World' BBC TV programme, uses high frequency superimposed on the normal supply to ionise the gap due to dirt on the track and restore electrical contact. The unit converts the 12 volt DC input into high frequency AC only when the circuit is broken, burning away the dirt and restoring conductivity. The normal DC current then flows again. The generator is easily wired into the layout input and is perfectly safe to use.

The Codar 'Steam-sound' electronic synthesiser.

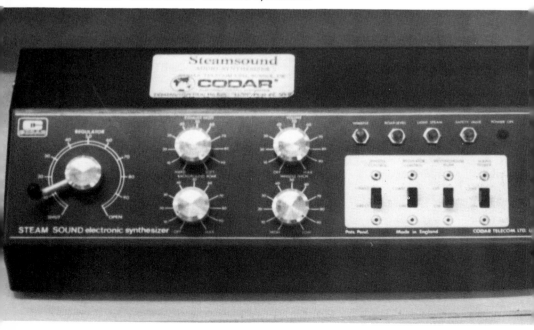

PSL MODEL RAILWAY GUIDE

2
Layout Planning

Michael Andress

 Patrick Stephens, Cambridge

Softbound edition first published September 1979
Reprinted November 1981
Reprinted February 1983

Combined casebound edition (with *PSL Model Railway Guide 1*) first published November 1981
Reprinted June 1982
Reprinted February 1983
Reprinted September 1983

ISBN 0-85059-359-X (softbound)
ISBN 0-85059-587-8 (combined casebound)

Cover photograph by Brian Monaghan, taken at the Wakefield Model Railway Society.

Text photoset in 8 on 9pt Univers by Stevenage Printing Limited, Stevenage. Printed in Great Britain on 90 gsm Fineblade coated cartridge and bound by The Garden City Press, Letchworth, for the publishers Patrick Stephens Limited, Bar Hill, Cambridge, CB3 8EL, England.

Contents

Introduction

Railway modelling is a very popular pastime with more enthusiasts taking up the hobby every year. Many of the newcomers start with a train set and the transition from this to a more permanent model railway layout is an important step for them. The scope of railway modelling is very wide indeed, ranging from the miniature engineering involved in constructing model locomotives, through the applications of electrical and electronic circuitry in model railway control, to the artistic aspects of structure and scenery modelling. The many different interests brought together in the hobby lead to great variety in the types of layouts built. This is one of the attractions of the hobby but the great choice can also be bewildering to the beginner who does not yet know where his special interests and skills may lie.

Railway modelling is also different from most other constructional hobbies in that we do not only model locomotives or trains just to be displayed as static items, or to be operated as individual models. Instead, our model represents a working railway complete with its surrounding landscape. This adds greatly to the interest. It also means that even though a layout may be complete enough for enjoyable running, construction can continue with the addition of extra models and details, and perhaps by extending the layout. The modeller can thus alternate construction and operation as he pleases, maintaining the interest and enthusiasm. In this way some layouts have been built up over many years and are now very large and elaborate. There is a danger that the beginner, when he sees pictures of these, may be tempted to tackle something too ambitious.

For the construction of a model railway layout which will continue to provide pleasure for the owner, some advance planning is necessary. It is also important to have some idea of what sort of layout is wanted. Often the beginner does not have the knowledge or experience to decide. My aim in this book is to give him some idea of the possibilities and to provide advice on the type of layout he can successfully tackle as a first project.

The term layout planning can be used in a rather restricted sense to describe the designing of the actual track arrangement, the number and positions of the platforms and other details. However, there is a great deal more than this for the modeller to consider in his planning and I want to use the term in a much wider context. We must decide on the size, shape, location and type of model railway layout and even the sort of structures and scenery which will be added. These, and other aspects, are all of importance in the creation of a satisfying model railway layout.

The book covers planning for 00-scale and N-scale layouts of types suitable for beginners. These are the most popular scales in this country, particularly 00, and are the ones best suited to the inexperienced modeller.

The ideas and information presented here are based on the experiences of many modellers. Over the years there have been many interesting developments in layout planning, particularly with regard to small layouts suitable for modern houses. Because an idea devised by one modeller is often modified and improved by others it is difficult to know how any particular scheme first originated. I would, however, like to give credit to the work of Cyril Freezer, now editor of *Model Railways* magazine, who has designed many interesting small layouts and who has done much to popularise the concept of branch line modelling.

I would like to thank all those modellers who have kindly allowed me to use photographs of their work to illustrate this book. In particular I am grateful to Graham Bailey, Tony Butler, Leo Campbell, K.J. Churms, Howard Coulson, Brian Dorman, Keith Gowen, David Hammersley, Dave Howsam, Terry Jenkins, Bob Jones, Ron Prattley, Phil Savage, Mike Sharman, Allan Sibley and Adrian Swain.

Some general considerations

Because we are modelling a whole system rather than just a few separate items which could be displayed on shelves or in a cabinet we must find space to accommodate our layout. To complete a model railway there are many models to be constructed or purchased and time and money will be required. Thus when deciding what sort of layout to build we must take into account the amount of space, time and money we can afford and also how long a period we are prepared to let the construction of the layout take. Obviously there is no point in planning a large and complex system if there is space for only a very small layout. What is often less evident to the beginner is the heavy commitment in hours of work and in cost involved in the building of a large model railway. Many

The Isle of Purbeck MRC 4 mm scale Swanage Branch layout was modelled very closely on the prototype line and is very realistic. However most modellers do not have the space or time to construct such a large layout and must compress and compromise much more.

Some general considerations

Part of the attractive DJH Models 00-scale demonstration layout which was constructed entirely from commercially available items. Note how the small factory utilises the space in the corner of the layout providing not only scenic interest but also a siding to add to the operating scope of the line.

really big layouts have been built over many years by modellers who have been able and willing to devote a great deal of time and money to the hobby. It is essential not to be too ambitious in the choice of a first layout. Later, if the modeller finds he can spare more space, time and money he can tackle a more extensive project.

The track design is very important in determining the appearance of a model railway and how it can be run so it should be planned with some care. However, do not worry too much about trying to make your plan perfect; it never will be! Your first layout is most unlikely to be your final one and, indeed, will probably be very different from what you eventually decide you want in a layout. As you gain knowledge and experience you will want to modify, improve, alter and extend your layout and later you will probably decide to scrap or sell it and build a new and better one, incorporating those features you have come to realise you want to include. So, while it is wise to give some thought to planning your model railway before starting construction, do not spend too long 'armchair modelling'—planning, designing and dreaming without actually building anything! There is no substitute for practical experience.

Though track planning will be discussed later in this book I would suggest that the beginner may well do best to choose a published plan, the basic design of which appeals to him, and to modify it as necessary to suit his own tastes, rather than try to make up his own plan. Small changes will give individuality to the published plan without affecting the essential features. In this way problems of design, some of which may only become apparent too late in construction for easy correction, will be avoided. Do not feel that you are showing a lack of originality by copying a plan in this way. There is only a limited number of workable schemes suitable for small layouts and most, if not all, of these must already have been utilised. Many track plans have been published in the model railway magazines, particularly in *Railway Modeller*, and Cyril Freezer has collected many of his layout plans into three books of which *60 Plans for Small Railways* is especially useful to the beginner.

When we plan a model railway we should always remember that the function of the prototype, with the exception now, perhaps, of the preserved lines, is to provide transportation. On some railways this is very specialised, for example, commuter lines carrying only passengers, mining railways transporting only ore; on others the traffic is mixed, with passengers, both long distance and local, and a wide variety of freight. If a model railway is to be realistic and interesting it should seem to be a replica of the real thing not only in appearance but also in operation. We can add variety to the running of the layout and to the rolling stock required by the provision of lineside industries, each with a siding or sidings to be shunted. There is an almost unlimited choice of possible industries, some of which require special types of rolling stock to serve them, and this is another way in which individuality can be introduced into your model railway.

The restrictions of space, time and money obviously limit what can be included on a layout. We have the choice of representing much of the prototype in outline only or of concentrating on a particular part and modelling it in much greater detail. Interesting layouts of both types have been built but model railways which specialise in an aspect in which the constructor is especially interested are usually more successful than those in which an attempt has been made to include almost everything. However, do remember that railway modelling is a hobby for your pleasure and enjoyment. Plan and build your layout the way you would like to have it and not how others tell you it ought to be. There are so many different aims, interests and ideas among railway modellers that the type of layout other enthusiasts like may not suit you at all. Your model railway is your own private little kingdom where you can express your own ideas and creativity,

and where you can make your own rules. Some enthusiasts will say that you must do this or that on your model because it is prototype practice to do so, but this is not necessarily a valid argument because we can never copy the real thing exactly anyway. Selection and compression are always needed and it is up to the individual to select the parts that he likes and which to him represent the best aspects of the prototype. Provided your layout gives you enjoyment and satisfaction it is a success!

The train set

The train set is the traditional introduction to railway modelling and it remains an excellent way of starting the hobby. The basic set usually consists of a locomotive, coaches or goods stock, and an oval of sectional track about 3½ ft × 2½ ft. Many different sets are produced with various combinations of steam, diesel or electric outline locomotive and coaches or goods vehicles. Some sets include additional track and one or more turnouts for sidings or a passing loop. Nowadays the models are generally of very good quality, they are accurate and well detailed and make an excellent basis from which to develop your layout. If the set is a gift the choice will already have been made for you, but if you are buying the train set yourself try to select a set which will not only meet your present needs but which will also

This simple first permanent layout was developed easily and quickly from a train set.

Some general considerations

be appropriate for your future layout. Your interests may change or become more specialised but it is obviously helpful if you have some idea of how you might want your railway to develop; if it is to follow British, American or European prototype, if it will be period steam or modern image diesel and so on. This may help to avoid the need for the replacement of locomotives and rolling stock at a later date.

Although it may be tempting to select a large and impressive express locomotive with main line coaches, a better choice is a small steam or diesel engine with a train of goods stock. A large locomotive will look out of place on a small layout with sharp curves, whereas a small engine will be equally at home on the train set oval or on the larger and more complex layout which you may build up from it eventually. I suggest goods vehicles as the initial items of rolling stock because they provide more opportunities for shunting when you add a few sidings. When you later acquire passenger stock, select short branch line coaches rather than full length main line stock. They will look better on sharp curves

and will allow you to use shorter platforms with a consequent saving in space.

Although the simple oval is convenient it has very limited operational scope. You can run a train clockwise or anti-clockwise around the track and that is all! While the oval is a useful basis for a small layout, providing as it does a continuous run in a small area, it needs additional features to make it more interesting. Even a single siding will permit us to drop off and pick up wagons. A run-around loop will give greater scope for shunting because the siding can then be worked by a train running in either direction. Further sidings provide additional permutations for shunting and extra interest. For example, we can represent a small industrial line with, perhaps, three sidings, each serving a factory or warehouse, and this will give considerable operating potential. As the track is sectional you can try out various

Eastern Models feature a timber works on their HO-scale demonstration layout. This industry is served by two sidings giving extra scope for shunting.

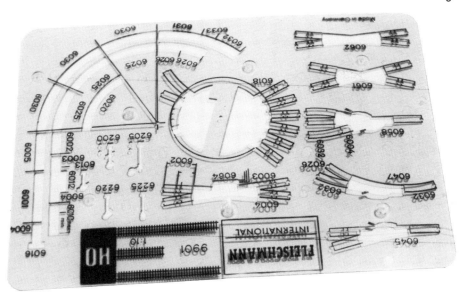

arrangements as you buy extra track and points. This can be a very valuable period of experimentation. There are many different ways of setting out the track and these will produce a variety of operating patterns. Running trains over these different track layouts may give you some idea of the sort of permanent layout you would like to build. You may, perhaps, enjoy watching the trains run steadily on a continuous line or you may prefer the challenge of shunting on a small, but complicated, industrial layout.

It is best to add gradually to the train set rather than to buy a lot of additional parts all at once. In this way you can experiment to the full with the track you have as you go along and you will have more idea of which extra pieces you would find most useful. Similarly with additional locomotives and rolling stock it is preferable to build up gradually from the basic set, so that you can, if you wish, change your mind about the type of railway you want without having to dispose of a lot of equipment, previously acquired but now unsuitable.

For a permanent model railway layout using flexible track a track plan is required as a guide, but it is more difficult to draw out a small scale plan for a layout using sectional track because it must be very accurate or the fixed pieces of sectional track may not fit

The Fleischmann HO-track stencil allows accurate planning to 1:10 scale of layouts with Fleischmann track pieces, points, crossings, etc.

when you come to lay the track. The easiest method is to lay it out full size using actual track pieces to make sure of the positioning. However, you may want to try out various designs on paper without having to buy the track sections until you decide on one particular plan, so that you can then buy just the pieces needed. Some manufacturers produce track stencils to enable the drawing up of accurate small scale plans of layouts which can be built using the sectional track which they make. They include Hornby (00 scale), Arnold (N scale) and Fleischmann (HO and N scales).

The train set has much to recommend it as a starting point for railway modellers. The sets are relatively inexpensive and you can build up from them gradually as your finances permit. The track is easy to assemble and provides good running; being sectional it allows the modeller to try out many different track layouts. The models are realistic and the train set can give a great deal of enjoyment as well as providing useful experience. It can be incorporated into a permanent layout later if you wish.

Some general considerations

Scale and Gauge

Some of the basic terms in railway modelling are often used rather loosely and the beginner may become confused by them. In view of this I feel that it is worthwhile first of all to explain the difference between scale and gauge and the relationship between 00 and HO scales and between Continental and British N scales.

Scale refers to the proportion between the prototype and the model. *Gauge* is the track width, measured between the inner surfaces of the running rails. The British prototype standard gauge is 4 ft 8 ½ in.

For 00 the scale is 4 mm to the foot; that is each foot on the prototype is represented by 4 mm on the model. Alternatively this can be expressed as a ratio of 1:76. The track gauge for 00 is 16.5 mm. HO scale is 3.5 mm to the foot or a ratio of 1:87, also with a track gauge of 16.5 mm. As we have two different scales with the same track gauge, representing in each case the standard 4 ft 8 ½ in gauge prototype, the track gauge must be incorrect for one of the scales. In fact it is in 00 scale that the track width is wrong, being narrower than it should be. This discrepancy arose soon after the commercial introduction of 00 gauge. At first it was intended that the scale should be half 0 scale, making it 3.5 mm to the foot with the virtually correct track gauge of 16.5 mm. However, manufacturers soon found that the small size of the British prototype loading gauge (the maximum permissible height and width for locomotives and rolling stock), compared to those in Europe and the United States, created two problems. The first was the difficulty of fitting the electric motors commercially produced at that time into the British prototype locomotives. The second concerned parts such as axle guards, bogie sides and locomotive valve gear. These parts had to be made thicker than scale to give them enough strength for commercially produced models. It was also necessary to increase clearance in proportion to the prototype to allow models to run on the sharp curves

needed on model railway layouts. The small British loading gauge allowed insufficient width for these increases and so the manufacturers adopted the slightly larger scale of 4 mm to the foot while retaining the 16.5 mm track gauge, the combination being named 00. With the development of smaller scales it is clear that the compromise is no longer necessary but manufacturers and modellers are now so heavily committed to 00 scale that a change to HO scale for British modelling is most unlikely. European and American manufacturers, with the benefits of the larger prototype loading gauges retained 3.5 mm scale and 16.5 mm gauge as HO scale.

00 in Britain and HO in Europe and America have become the most popular of all scales and this is reflected in the vast ranges of ready-to-run equipment, kits of all types, and parts which are produced. These scales are a good compromise in size, being small enough for an interesting layout to be built in a reasonable space, but large enough for good detailing and for relatively easy kit construction and scratch-building. The models are also easy to handle. The convenience of having such a wide variety of products on the market should not be underestimated. It means that a layout can be fairly quickly brought to the stage where it can be operated, whereas progress would be much slower if many of the items had to be hand-built, and the delay might then cause the modeller to lose interest and enthusiasm, particularly if he is a beginner. The proprietary models used to complete the layout initially can be replaced later by more detailed kits or scratch-built items if desired. Another advantage of the availability of good quality commercial products is that the modeller has more time to concentrate on those aspects of the hobby which interest him most. In addition the large potential market for products in 00 and HO scales encourages manufacturers to offer models of less popular prototypes and of more specialised items which in other scales could

not be profitably produced. Thus the modeller has a wider choice. The greater opportunities for mass production also means that the models may be less expensive.

Most modellers of British prototypes are prepared to accept the incorrect scale/ gauge ratio of 00 for the convenience and advantages of the large range of commercial items on the market, and so that their models will be compatible with those of their friends. If you find the slightly narrow gauge appearance of 4 mm scale on 16.5 mm gauge unacceptable you can model to EM scale (4 mm scale on 18 mm gauge) or to the exact Protofour standards (4 mm scale on 18.83 mm gauge) but either will involve you in more conversion and construction work than is necessary in 00 scale.

N scale was introduced commercially in the early 1960s by the German firm Arnold, with models to a ratio of 1:160, representing a scale of approximately 1.9 mm to the foot, running on track of 9 mm gauge. Unfortunately, for exactly the same reason that British prototypes were modelled to 00 scale instead of HO, it was considered necessary for the slightly larger scale of 2 1/16 mm to the foot, a ratio of 1:148, to be used for commercially produced models of British locomotives and rolling stock, and this has become the standard for British N scale. The track gauge is the same as for Continental and American N scale—9 mm.

N scale is well established and is now second only to 00 and HO scales in popularity. It offers a significant space advantage over the larger scales. A wide variety of models is available and the range of ready-to-run equipment, kits and parts is steadily increasing all the time. N scale has the advantage that standards for track, wheels and couplings were established early on so that all the models produced are compatible in these respects. Thus the modeller does not have the expense or trouble of having to change wheels or couplings to match his own equipment. The present N-scale standards for wheels and track are rather coarse in comparison to those in the larger scales. This makes for reliable running but does detract from the appearance. There have been moves to introduce finer scale standards in N scale and it may be that the manufacturers will adopt these eventually.

I have discussed 00 and N scales in some detail because these are the scales the beginner is most likely to choose; I would certainly recommend that one of these be selected. Of course the choice may already have been made by the gift or purchase of a train set, by the gift of some equipment from a railway modelling friend, or because someone you know has a layout and you want to work to the same scale.

If you have not yet decided I suggest you look at the models in the shops, at exhibitions, or on a friend's layout to see which scale appeals most to you. You might even like to buy one or two kits and make them up to see how you find working in the different scales before you commit yourself too far to want to change. 00 scale has the advantage of being less fiddly to handle and kit construction and scratch-building tend to be easier because of the larger size. Though, conversely, some workers in N scale claim that as less detail is required they find it easier to build models in the smaller scale than in 00. Really it all comes down to your own preferences and to getting used to modelling in any particular scale. The small size of N scale may make it possible for you to fit a more interesting layout into the space you have available. The choice is up to you depending on the circumstances and on your personal feelings about the appearance and feel of the models. Do not make the mistake of thinking that it will be cheaper to model in the smaller N scale! The locomotive and rolling stock models tend to be fairly similar in price in 00 and N scales for comparable quality because the expense of manufacture is much the same. In fact an N-scale layout may well cost you more because you can fit so much more into the same space than on an 00-scale model railway.

Definitions

As I have already indicated I feel that the beginner should start with 00 or N scale. The following brief listing of scales and gauges is provided for general interest and information and so that you will be familiar with them when you see them mentioned in model railway magazines, rather than because I am suggesting other alternative scales for the beginner. Later, after experience in 00 or N scale, the modeller may wish to try out another scale and by then he will be in a better position to assess what this will involve.

Z scale (1.4 mm to the foot or 1:220; 6.5 mm gauge; prototype gauge equivalent 4 ft 8 1/4 in).

This is the most recently introduced commercial scale. The models, by Märklin, are remarkably well detailed but are expensive and only Continental prototypes are

Scale and Gauge

produced. A few plastic structure kits are made for this scale by Kibri.

N Scale — US and Continental (1.9 mm to the foot or 1:160; 9 mm gauge; prototype gauge equivalent 4 ft 8½ in).

Now well established and second only to HO scale in popularity in America and Europe. There is a wide range of ready-to-run models of high quality with the advantage that wheel and rail standards are generally uniform and that there is a universal coupling, so that stock from different manufacturers can be run together. Many kits and parts are also marketed.

N Scale — British (2¹⁄₁₆ mm to the foot or 1:148; 9 mm gauge; prototype gauge equivalent 4 ft 4½ in).

This is also now very popular being second only to 00 scale in Britain. There is a reasonable selection of ready-to-run locomotives and rolling stock and a steadily increasing range of kits, including a variety of cast metal locomotive body kits to fit onto commercial chassis. Many structures and accessories are now on the market, either ready-made or in kit form. The large range of excellent Continental structure kits can also be utilised, sometimes with minor modifications to make them appear more British. These European kits are strictly speaking slightly underscale for British N-scale layouts but this is not really noticeable in practice and can even be an advantage, particularly in the case of large buildings, as the structures will occupy a little less space than if they were to exact scale.

000 Scale (2 mm to the foot or 1:152; 9.5 mm gauge; prototype gauge equivalent 4 ft 8½ in).

This is a scale for the enthusiast who is prepared to hand-build most of his models himself and it is not suitable for inexperienced workers. There is an active 2 mm Scale Association which provides considerable assistance for modellers working in this scale.

TT Scale — Continental (2.5 mm to the foot or 1:120; 12 mm gauge; prototype gauge equivalent 4 ft 8½ in).

There has been a revival of interest in this scale in Germany recently with the re-introduction of the old East German Zeuke products in revised and improved form as Berliner Bahnen. This firm offers a good range of locomotives and rolling stock and also figures and road vehicles.

TT Scale — British (TT3) (3 mm to the foot or 1:100; 12 mm gauge; prototype gauge equivalent 4 ft).

Though the scale received a setback with the introduction of N scale and no ready-to-run models are at present made, there is still a range of kits and parts available and modellers are supported by an active association, the 3 mm Society, which produces its own magazine *Mixed Traffic* for its members. The scale offers a compromise between 00 and N scales but the lack of ready-to-run equipment makes it unsuitable for the beginner.

HO Scale (3.5 mm to the foot or 1:87; 16.5 mm gauge; prototype gauge equivalent 4 ft 8½ in).

The most popular scale by far in the United States and on the Continent with a very extensive range of ready-to-run equipment, kits, parts and accessories.

00 Scale (4 mm to the foot or 1:76; 16.5 mm gauge; prototype gauge equivalent 4 ft 1½ in).

The most popular scale in Britain with many advantages for the beginner despite the inaccurate scale/gauge ratio.

EM gauge (18 mm gauge with 4 mm to the foot scale; prototype gauge equivalent 4 ft 6 in) gives a much better appearance and track is now available from Ratio, though locomotives and rolling stock must be modified by the modeller. The EM Gauge Society provides assistance for workers in this gauge.

Protofour — P4 (18.83 mm gauge with 4 mm to the foot scale; prototype gauge equivalent 4 ft 8½ in). This is a system with an exact scale/track gauge ratio and also a set of fine scale standards for track, wheels and other details. The Protofour Society provides advice and information and a number of items are now commercially available for the system. The results are excellent but the beginner should acquire experience with 00 scale first.

S Scale ($\frac{3}{16}$ in to the foot or 1:64; $\frac{7}{8}$ in gauge; prototype gauge equivalent 4 ft 8 in).

There are some commercial items available for this scale in the United States but not in Britain. It is a useful compromise between 00 and 0 scales but is not suitable for the beginner because models must be hand-built.

0 Scale — British (7 mm to the foot or 1:43; 32 mm gauge; prototype gauge equivalent 4 ft 7 in).

An attractive scale because of the size and weight of the models and the detail which can be included, but generally not suitable for the beginner because of the expense involved and the space needed. There are a number of inexpensive locomotives and rolling stock models of Continental manufacture available, some of British prototype, but the range is very limited.

1 Scale (10 mm to the foot or 1:30.5; 45 mm gauge; prototype gauge equivalent 4 ft 6 in).

Even more expensive in space and cost than 0 scale. There is a range of ready-to-run locomotives and rolling stock of Continental prototype from Märklin.

Narrow gauge

Narrow-gauge modelling has become very popular in recent years, partly because of the numerous preserved lines now in operation but mainly due to the introduction of commercial ready-to-run models, kits and parts in some scales. A railway is narrow gauge if its track width is less than the standard 4 ft 8 ½ in, but most modellers tend to choose prototypes of metre gauge or less. Apart from the undoubted charm of these railways there are advantages for the modeller because the sharp curves, steep gradients, small locomotives, short trains and simple stations typical of narrow-gauge lines enable a model to be built in a smaller space than a standard-gauge model railway would need.

If we set out to model a narrow-gauge prototype we can use one of the commercially produced gauges and choose the appropriate scale to go with it or we can decide on the scale we will model to and make the gauge to suit. Generally it is best to employ a recognised gauge so that commercial wheels, mechanisms and, if desired, track can be used. If the scale and gauge are chosen so that the scale is also one which is catered for by the trade we have the ideal arrangement. We can use items such as structures, figures, road vehicles, and other accessories from the scale chosen while employing wheels, mechanisms, bogies and so on from the smaller scale which has the gauge we are using.

The following are the most usual scale/gauge combinations:

Nn3 (N scale on Z gauge representing 3 ft gauge prototype). I have not heard of any modellers in Britain using this combination so far but a few American enthusiasts have built narrow-gauge layouts in N scale using locomotives and rolling stock converted from Märklin Z-scale models. Unfortunately the high cost of the Z-scale models is likely to deter many modellers but the combination has considerable potential for the modeller who would like an extensive narrow-gauge system in a limited space.

00n2 and HOn2½ (These are respectively 4 mm scale (usually known as 009) and 3.5 mm scale (usually known as HO9 or HOe) on 9 mm gauge track). Strictly speaking the former is equivalent to 2 ft 3 in gauge prototype and the latter approximately 2 ft 6 in but both are used to model prototypes of from 2 ft to 2 ft 6 in gauge. Some ready-to-run models of Continental prototype are available and a variety of British kits are produced including cast metal locomotive body kits to fit onto N-gauge commercial chassis. The modeller can also utilise N-scale locomotive mechanisms, wagon underframes and wheels, coach bogies and so on for his own models. 009 track and points are made by Peco, or N-scale track can be used if the sleepers, which are wrongly spaced, are largely hidden by the ballast. The latter choice enables the modeller to benefit from the more extensive range of points, crossings and other special track available in N scale. Lilliput make a useful dual-gauge (16.5 mm and 9 mm) crossing for 00- or HO-scale layouts which have both standard- and narrow-gauge track.

HOn3 (This is 3.5 mm scale on 10.5 mm gauge track for 3 ft gauge prototypes). It is popular in the United States where brass ready-to-run locomotives and rolling stock, numerous parts and a variety of rolling stock kits are on sale. Ready-made track is also produced. Some of these items are available in Britain from specialist model railway shops.

00n3 (4 mm scale on 12 mm gauge representing 3 ft gauge prototype). Gem in Britain market a number of metal kits for the Isle of Man Railway equipment and TT3 mechanisms and other parts can be used also.

HOm (3.5 mm scale on 12 mm gauge track for metre gauge prototypes). This scale/gauge combination was formerly catered for by Zeuke of East Germany but ready-to-run locomotives and rolling stock together with sectional and flexible track and points are now produced by Bemo.

0n2¼ (7 mm scale on 16.5 mm gauge track; equivalent to approximately 2 ft 4 in gauge prototype but used to represent gauges of 2 ft 3 in and 2 ft 6 in also). This is an attractive combination as the models are large enough to allow considerable detailing but a layout can be built in the same space as a comparable one in 00 scale. The vast range of mechanisms, wheels, underframes and track parts intended for 00 and HO can be used for convenience and economy and there is a good selection of accessories such as figures and road vehicles for 0 scale. The

Scale and Gauge

Peco locomotive and rolling stock cast metal kits for this scale/gauge combination should help to make it popular.

On2½ (¼ in to the foot scale on 16.5 mm gauge track). This is the American equivalent of the above and has similar advantages.

10 mm, 14 mm and 16 mm scales on 32 mm gauge track (Representing respectively 3 ft, 2 ft 3 in and 2 ft gauge prototypes). The large size of these models means that they can be very well detailed. Some modellers have used the inexpensive Triang Big Big Train (0 gauge) locomotives and rolling stock as a basis for models to these scales. The Triang models are no longer produced but they can sometimes be obtained second hand. Some accessories are available in 10 mm scale and others can be adapted from military modelling kits.

G-gauge (14 mm scale on 45 mm gauge track). The LGB range of ready-to-run locomotives and rolling stock is quite extensive and is being steadily enlarged. The manufacturer also makes sectional track and points to complete the system. The models are mainly of European prototypes but a few American models are also made. The scale/gauge combination is equivalent to metre gauge.

Broad gauge

The broad-gauge prototypes have not become popular for modelling in the way that the narrow-gauge railways have, though a few layouts have been built featuring models of the Irish 5 ft 3 in gauge railways. Mike Sharman has modelled the old Brunel 7 ft gauge very effectively on his superb Victorian period 4 mm scale layout which also includes standard- and narrow-gauge tracks together with some complex mixed gauge trackwork. Mike Sharman also offers a number of cast metal kits commercially for broad-gauge modelling in 4 mm scale.

A layout built by Terry Jenkins. This 00-scale model railway is typical of the sort of layout a beginner can tackle successfully. The structures are mainly modified kits and the scenic work is straightforward but effective.

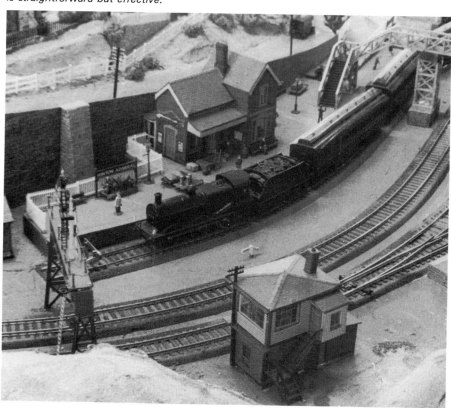

Layout size

I have already cautioned the beginner not to be tempted, by seeing large and elaborate model railways, into tackling something too ambitious for his first layout. It is also very easy when studying layout plans drawn to a small scale to underestimate the size that these layouts will be when built. When considering a plan it is a good idea to measure out on the floor the dimensions of the layout so that you can visualise more easily how much space it would occupy. Even a 6 ft × 4 ft layout, usually classified as small, will take up quite a lot of a small or medium sized room, and if you need to carry it at all, you will find it surprisingly massive.

The beginner sometimes has the belief that if a small layout will be good then a large one must be even better! This is quite wrong. A model railway does not have to be large and elaborate to be successful. Indeed, the greatest entertainment comes from a layout when it is fully used and as most modellers usually operate single-handed the layout should not be too big.

There are many advantages in building a small layout as your first model railway. As I indicated earlier the three basic limiting factors when constructing a layout are the time, money and space which we are able and willing to afford. For a small layout the initial financial outlay will be low, particularly if the modeller is progressing from a train set and already has much of the equipment he needs. The further costs incurred during construction will also be small and there will be no danger of progress being held up through lack of money.

Because only a limited number of models can be accommodated on a small layout the modeller can afford to make sure they are of a high standard, either by purchasing more expensive models or by taking the time to build well detailed ones himself. In the relatively small area, progress on scenic work will be encouragingly good for only a few evenings of modelling, and there is again time to attend to all the small details which

make a layout more interesting.

A model railway is a working model and if it is to provide the maximum enjoyment for its owner it must work well. Good track and wiring are essential and it is much easier both to construct and to maintain smooth, accurate track and good electrical contact on a small layout than on a large one, simply because there is so much less of it.

Often lack of space limits the size of layout which can be built and the modeller has no alternative but to settle for a small model railway. However, even if a large area is available it is still advisable to start out modestly. If the plan is chosen with some forethought a small simple layout, which can be completed fairly quickly and easily, can later be extended or incorporated into a larger system. If possible select the site for your layout with this in mind. Many excellent layouts have been developed in this way. John Allen's HO scale 'Gorre & Daphetid', one of the finest model railroads ever constructed, started out as a small layout approximately 6½ ft × 3½ ft in size and this original section was retained, with only minor alterations, as part of the eventually very large and complex system.

Alternatively, when the layout has been completed and has provided all the operating entertainment it can, you may decide to scrap it rather than use it as part of a larger layout. It may be that your ideas have changed and that it will be easier to build a completely new layout as you want it rather than to try to alter the old one. The standard of your modelling work may also have improved so that the original section is no longer up to the standard you want. Though the beginner tends to think of his first layout, while he is planning and building it, as his final one, most modellers do construct more than one layout, in many cases several. This is another advantage of starting with a small layout as you will be more likely to scrap it and start again than if you are heavily committed in time and money to a large layout. Scrapping a small layout is not the extravagance it may seem. The original cost of the layout will have been amply repaid in the pleasure and experience you have gained in building and operating it and many of the parts, perhaps even the baseboard, can be saved and re-used. A fresh start may also stimulate your interest and enthusiasm.

For the beginner I would suggest a layout no larger than about 6 ft × 4 ft for a rectangular layout accommodating a continuous run track plan of some type. If possible it is best to have a central operating well in layouts of this sort. Access to all parts of the layout is then much easier, particularly as it will probably be necessary to have one side of the layout against a wall. The model railway also appears much more realistic to operate as the trains look as if they are really going somewhere rather than just round and round. This seems to be because you have to turn to watch the train as it passes behind you instead of being able to see it all the time from one position as you can when you view the layout from one side.

For a long narrow layout for a point-to-point design, perhaps as an L-shape fitting into the corner of a room, a baseboard with arms of up to about 6 or 8 ft long and 1-2 ft wide is the maximum size I would advise for a first layout.

The track plan for whatever type of layout is selected should be fairly simple with relatively few points. This is important because the number of points included on a layout influences considerably the time taken to build and later to maintain the model railway.

Even if you anticipate that the layout will be a permanent fitting in the room there is much to be said for constructing it as a number of units, each preferably no larger than about 4 ft × 2ft, which can be fixed together rigidly but which can be taken apart if necessary for storage or transportation. Obviously for a portable layout some arrangement of this sort will be essential.

I believe it was Cyril Freezer who once wrote that it is easier to build a good small layout than a good large layout. This is a very true statement and one which all beginners would do well to keep in mind!

Layout location

When planning a layout the beginner may well look around the house trying to find a large space for his model railway. I can remember planning a grandiose scheme and then looking for the largest possible site to accommodate it, but fortunately as a

beginner I never got as far as actually trying to build my dream layout! These larger spaces include sites such as the loft, the garage or a garden shed and all of these have been utilised very satisfactorily by many modellers. As an example, Mike Sharman's large mixed gauge period layout is now being built into the owner's loft. However, Mike is an expert modeller with great experience, capable not only of constructing a large layout on which almost everything is hand-built but also of fitting out his loft to house the railway. It is worth mentioning though that his layout began as a much smaller portable section which has since been incorporated into the present system.

Personally, I would not recommend any of the above sites for the beginner. Generally I do not feel it is the right approach at this stage because in an effort to obtain the use of a space which is probably much larger than is required the modeller is accepting some serious disadvantages. For example, it can be very dusty in a garage, making operation troublesome and causing problems in maintenance. Fitting out a loft or erecting a garden shed may involve so much work and cost that the modeller may never actually get round to building the layout which was the real object of the exercise! All these sites are likely to be cold in winter, so you will either end up not using the layout then or providing heating which will add to the expense. On wet nights the idea of going out to a garden shed to run your railway is not very inviting! There is also the danger that, having created a large space exclusively for a model railway, the modeller may be tempted to start on too large a layout. I also feel that it is a pity to isolate yourself from the rest of the family while working on or running your railway.

Now I know there are exceptions to the comments I have made above. A friend of mine who lived in a bungalow had a fully fitted-out loft with easy access already, so he erected his portable layout in the centre of the loft and used the rest to store his kits, tools, books and so on. In this case the loft was really the equivalent of a spare room and my objections about work needed for fitting out and lack of comfort do not apply. However, most of us are not so fortunate and in general I think it is best to try to find a site within the main part of the house. There are many places in most houses where a small layout of the sort a beginner should be tackling can be accommodated. Indeed successful layouts have been built in small flats, bedsitters and even a caravan!

If you are lucky enough to have a spare

room which can be devoted exclusively to your hobby then there is no problem. More frequently, however, the layout must be accommodated in a room which will be used for other purposes also and it must not interfere unduly with these other activities. Often a youngster will want to develop his train set into a permanent continuous-run layout on a baseboard in his bedroom. A rectangular baseboard of this type does occupy a considerable part of the free area of a room even if its size is kept to a minimum. As it will almost certainly need to be pushed back against a wall, a baseboard with a central operating well is the best arrangement so that access to the whole layout is easy. Unfortunately there is a tendency for a layout like this in a bedroom to become untidy. The models themselves get dusty and things may be left on and under the baseboard making cleaning up difficult. A neat solution to the problem is to arrange the baseboard so that it folds up against one wall when the layout is not in use, leaving the room clear. The layout should be hinged along one edge onto a strong frame fixed firmly to the wall. Shelves or cupboards can be built into the lower part of the frame below the layout to store the locomotives and rolling stock between operating sessions. Hinging the layout in this way does involve additional construction work but it may mean that a layout can be built in a room where it would not otherwise be acceptable. It also ensures that the layout is kept tidy, because

loose models, tools and so on, must be removed before the baseboard is folded up. There will also be more protection from dust and accidental damage for the layout.

An alternative way of installing a permanent layout in a room is to fit a long, narrow baseboard along one or more walls. The most suitable arrangement for the beginner is a layout limited to only one or two of the walls. In this way the door of the room can be left clear avoiding the need for any form of lifting section to be included. This type of layout can conveniently be supported on storage units; many suitable pieces of furniture are available at very reasonable prices from discount stores, either as ready-made units or in kit form for home assembly. If preferred, the baseboard can be fixed to the wall as a shelf. A neat and convenient method is to use one of the slotted shelving systems obtainable from DIY shops. A layout of this type can be fitted into a bedroom with very little effect on the usual purposes of the room. Similarly, if an along-the-wall layout is very neatly finished it may be acceptable in the lounge. If you are really stuck for space do not overlook the possibility of installing a narrow layout along the wall in the hall. In many houses the hall is too small for this but in others there would be ample, otherwise wasted, space.

If you fit a layout into the lounge you may like to have a cover so the layout will be concealed when not in use. This will also protect the model from dust and damage.

A close view of part of a neat 00-scale bookcase layout built by Dave Howsam and Ron Prattley showing the goods yard. Layout is realistic and interesting even though actual width available is only 10½ in. (Photo by Ron Prattley.)

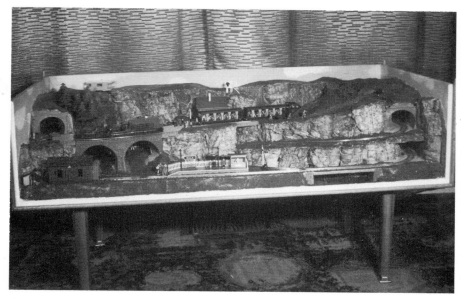

An interesting 009 narrow-gauge layout built in a coffee table. Design is essentially a dog bone with the loops overlapped. (Model, photo and plan by K.J. Churms.)

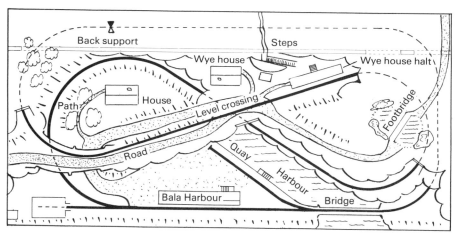

Dave Howsam and Ron Prattley have constructed a very neat bookcase to house a terminus to fiddle yard design model railway. When not in use the model is hidden and the unit looks like a typical bookcase. To set up for operating, the top is removed to reveal the terminus on the fixed part of the bookcase. The top is reversed and fitted onto one end of the unit where it forms the remainder of the layout, including the fiddle yard. The complete layout measures 16 ft in length. The bookcase also provides useful

bookshelves and cupboards. An advantage of a unit of this type is that it is free standing and does not require any fixing to the wall as would be needed with a shelf layout. If a more extensive layout is wanted further units can be constructed to carry the railway along a second wall as well. Dave and Ron built their bookcase up from wood and chipboard, but you may well be able to find suitable units, either ready-made or in kit form, which could be adapted for this purpose.

If you do not want to tackle the

An L-shaped portable N-scale layout following German prototype. The model which includes a double-track mainline and a single-track branchline is not yet complete, requiring two further sections at the right-hand end. When not in use the layout breaks down into four sections which can be easily carried and stored.

One of the sections of the German N-scale layout. Three of the units, including this one, measure 40 in × 20 in, the other section is 60 in × 20 in. The modules are bolted together to assemble the layout.

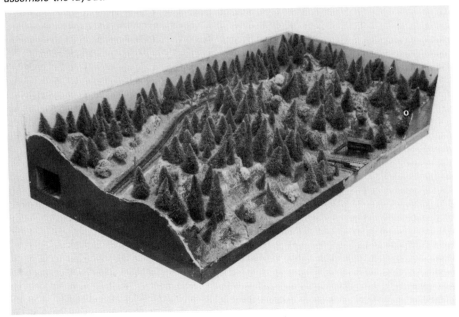

Layout size

construction of a unit as large as a bookcase, but would like a railway layout that can be kept in the lounge, you might consider building a coffee table layout. These very small layouts in 009, N or Z scale usually measure about 3 ft × 1½ or 2 ft, and have a continuous run track plan, either an oval or a figure of eight design. The model is built into a coffee table the top, and sometimes also the sides, of which are plate glass. Obviously the scope of such a layout is limited, but nevertheless the construction can provide good experience in everything from track laying to scenic detailing. As can be seen from the layout shown, constructed by K.J. Churms, the finished result can be a very attractive piece of furniture and it will certainly promote interest in railway modelling!

For the modeller with limited space, particularly if his accommodation may not be permanent, a portable layout can be the answer. The layout is made up of a number of sections, each of which should be a maximum of 4 ft × 2 ft, which are set up for operating sessions and stored away afterwards. It is important that they are stored neatly both to keep them out of the way and to avoid damage. Keith Gowen's TT-scale branch line layout is a portable model railway and is stored in a large cupboard when not in use; this is a very convenient scheme and if you have a suitable cupboard it would be worth making your layout sections the correct size to fit into it. An advantage of a portable layout is that construction work can be carried out very conveniently as each section is small and, not being fixed down, can be carried to the workbench or a table. In this way you can work on the model in comfort and under ideal conditions.

The idea of constructing the layout as a series of sections has been taken rather further by some modellers, particularly in the United States. These enthusiasts often build a number of separate units or modules completing each one fully, even to the smallest details, before going on. In some cases the modules offer little or no possibility for operation at the time and are intended more as a convenient way for a modeller without much space to enjoy construction. Eventually if space for a layout becomes available the modeller will have several modules which can be fitted together as the basis of a layout. The module method of building also has some advantages for the beginner in that he can practise construction techniques and enjoy a variety of work on a small unit. Obviously this method does not provide much scope for those interested in operation, though if you can run trains on a club layout or one belonging to a friend you might like to consider it as a way of enjoying construction at home. The modules can be made to a standard size for convenience in building and storage, but need not be the same.

A further step has been taken in the United States with N scale with a system called N-Track. A number of modellers are building standard size modules on which the tracks are arranged so that they are in set positions at the ends of each module. This enables any module to be joined to any other. Standards such as the minimum radius for curves are also set. The system allows units to be linked to form large layouts for exhibitions or for operating sessions when several modellers get together.

Market Redwing station on Keith Gowen's TT-scale portable layout. Neat modelling has resulted in a very realistic appearance. Note the token exchange apparatus in the lower left corner of the picture.

Track schemes

There are only a few basic track designs and all layouts employ one or more of these. The best known, from its train set origin is the oval. It is a very useful arrangement but its appearance must be disguised if it is to be realistic. Concealing part of the oval with scenery is desirable. Part of the toy-like look of the train set oval is due to its symmetry and distorting the oval will help to disguise its nature. Positioning the tracks so that they are not parallel with the edge of the baseboard will also improve the appearance. Often straight track can be replaced by a gently curving line, again showing greater realism. The layout will also look much more realistic if viewed from within the oval by providing a central operating well. The oval gives a continuous run on which the train can travel as long as you wish without the need to stop, turn or reverse and this can be very convenient, especially if you just enjoy watching your models run.

The figure of eight layout provides a greater length of run per lap in the same area as an oval. However it either involves a track crossing at the same level, a feature more typical of US prototypes than on British lines, or at different levels. For a realistic figure of eight layout the scenery must be planned to justify the track arrangements and gradients. This is best done with hills, rivers and other natural obstacles.

The oval—the simplest continuous run design, derived from the train set.

The figure of eight design with tracks crossing on different levels.

 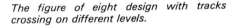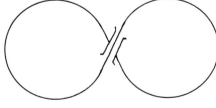

The one level figure of eight design with track crossing provides more length of run per lap than the oval.

The twice around track plan which provides almost double the length of run of the oval in the same area.

Track schemes

If the design is twisted further a twice around, continuous run plan results. This is a very useful arrangement as it gives about twice the length of run per lap of a simple oval, but again the scenery must be designed to make the track design appear plausible. With a plan of this type it is best to avoid having too much exactly parallel track as this will make the layout less realistic.

The dog bone is a variant of the oval.

Another form of continuous run scheme is the dog bone, essentially an oval with the sides brought closer together. It can be extended and twisted on itself to give a much longer run. As the two sides of the dog bone can be brought together to resemble double track this design can be used for a main line layout. The loops are the least realistic parts and are best concealed; it may be possible to place one above the other and hide them both together thus saving space on the layout.

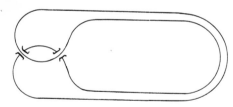

The folded dog bone provides greater length of run. Positioning one loop above the other, either partly as here or completely, saves space.

An entirely different arrangement is the point-to-point track plan. Whereas the oval is derived from the train set, this scheme is based on the prototype resulting in realism and authenticity. The only major disadvantage of the point-to-point layout is that the length of run for the train is limited. The usual design for this kind of layout is a long, narrow one, often running along one or more walls of a room. However, a point-to-point layout design can be twisted on itself into a spiral to

The point-to-point scheme, here as a straight design is often bent into an L-shape to fit into the corner of a room extending along two walls, and can also be bent further into a U-shape to fit onto a rectangular baseboard.

fit onto an ordinary rectangular baseboard. One terminus on a point-to-point layout may take the form of a fiddle yard.

A variant is the out and back scheme in which one terminus (or the fiddle yard in a terminus to fiddle yard design) is replaced by a loop so that the train is brought back to the terminus from which it started. This is a useful arrangement, particularly if the loop is combined with an oval so that the train can

A variant on the point-to-point scheme is the out and back design where the fiddle yard, or one terminus, is replaced by a reversing loop. This design can also be twisted to fit onto a rectangular baseboard.

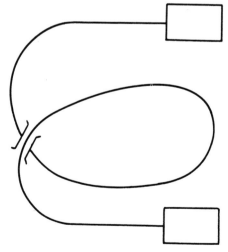

Further twisting results in a spiral point-to-point design giving greater length of run.

make as many laps around the oval as desired before coming back to the terminus. It does, however, require a special wiring arrangement for the reversing loop part of the system. An out and back design can be built on a long, narrow board—though a wider part will be needed to accommodate the loop. Alternatively, the track plan can be twisted into a spiral or figure of eight shape to fit on a shorter, wider rectangular baseboard. A more elaborate reversing loop with extra tracks acting as hidden sidings will make for more interesting operation by allowing the order in which the trains return to the terminus to be varied from that in which they left it.

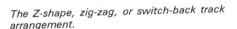

The Z-shape, zig-zag, or switch-back track arrangement.

An entirely different concept in track planning is the Z-shaped or switchback arrangement. Here a greater length of run for the trains is achieved by having three tracks form a Z-shape, each track being nearly the full length of the baseboard. In fact even more than three tracks can be included if desired. On such a layout the train travels three times the length of the layout (if three tracks are used) and the interest of operation is further increased by the reversing that is needed. Obviously, for the sake of reality we must introduce a good reason for the presence of three parallel tracks. On a small industrial layout the excuse may be that the track arrangement is needed to provide access to all the various factories, warehouses and other industries. Another way in which the scheme can be justified is to provide vertical separation between the tracks. For example on a mining layout a switchback track arrangement can be employed to bring the railway down the hillside in a situation where we can claim that it would have been too difficult or expensive for the prototype to have built curves to bring the line down in one continuous run. The scenery on such a layout must be rugged enough to support this argument. Though the beginner is perhaps best advised to build a single level layout for his first attempt, the switchback design on different levels has some interesting features and is worthy of consideration if lack of space forces you to build a narrow layout. This scheme does not

appear to have been used much in Britain but is more popular in America.

It is of course possible to combine more than one of the basic track arrangements in one layout. For example, a continuous oval plan with a branch leading to a terminus combines the oval and point-to-point types.

Your choice of basic scheme will be influenced by your interests. If you enjoy watching your trains run in a realistic landscape, pick a simple continuous design—do not put in too much track and hide some of the track you have in tunnels and behind hills. If you are more interested in shunting then a point-to-point, or a Z-shaped design with lineside industries to shunt, will probably appeal more.

Basic concepts—Fiddle yards

The idea of the fiddle yard is one which has largely developed with the concept of the branch line point-to-point model railway layout. In the restricted space often available for this type of railway, rather than have two limited terminal stations unrealistically close together it was felt better to concentrate on constructing one rather more interesting terminus. The other end of the line was then led to some hidden sidings which represented the rest of the railway system. At first these sidings were provided with a run around arrangement and were operated much as a normal station would be. Sometimes a turntable was included to allow the engine to be reversed. However, as the sidings were hidden from view anyway, modellers soon found it quicker and more convenient to ignore prototype practice and to provide merely a bank of storage sidings on which the locomotives and rolling stock were rearranged by hand. Hence the name 'fiddle yard'. This is a most useful device as it allows reversal and rearrangement of trains easily and quickly while using a minimum of space. In fact the yard can often be made detachable so that it is fitted onto the layout during operating sessions only. In this way it increases the rolling stock capacity of the railway and makes operation more interesting. An alternative arrangement to a bank of sidings fed by points is the provision of a traverser table with a single track lead. The table is moved to give access to its sidings. Such a traverser need not be elaborate, but merely a simple sliding board moved by hand, with spring brass contacts for electrical supply to the tracks.

Finding that the rearrangement of trains in the fiddle yard was a rather uninteresting chore for one operator on his well known

Track schemes

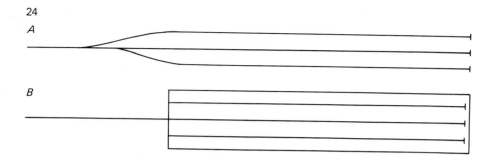

Fiddle yards. Typical fiddle yard (a). A traverser fiddle yard (b). Fiddle yard on concealed part of oval (c).

'Buckingham Branch' layout, Peter Denny devised an ingenious detachable 5 track fiddle yard. When all the trains have entered the fiddle yard it is detached, turned end for end reversing all the trains at once, and replaced. Small end doors are slid in to prevent any stock falling from the yard during turning. Operation can then immediately continue. This method has the additional bonus that stock can be stored in the fiddle yard when the layout is not in use. Not only is the stock kept safe from damage but the trains are ready for running as soon as the yard is fixed onto the layout. The Rev Denny has since further developed his fiddle yard by arranging for reversal without detaching. With a mechanism based on Meccano parts the yard is designed to move away a short distance to give clearance, and the whole fiddle yard then rotates as a train turntable to reverse it. The yard is then moved in again to meet the layout.

An alternative to a fiddle yard for turning trains is to use a series of reversing loop tracks but this requires much more space.

A most ingenious form of fiddle yard has been devised by an American modeller, in the form of a train ferry. The model ferry is mounted on a wheeled cart, very much like an old wooden tea trolley, which he has constructed to match the height of his layout. The trains are run onto the ferry which then 'sails' by being wheeled away on its cart. The ferry could be double ended so

that it could be wheeled back into place with the trains reversed. Again, a ferry fiddle yard can be used for storage, and there will also be space for storage on the trolley underneath it. Plans for a 4 mm scale train ferry are included in the range of Skinley Blueprints and would enable a modeller to construct a realistic model of a British ferry.

Though fiddle yards and hidden sidings are particularly associated with point-to-point branchline layouts they can also be usefully employed to add operating potential to layouts based on other track patterns. For example, the rear of an oval can be concealed and sidings can be provided here for train holding or for use as a fiddle yard. Similarly on an out and back scheme hidden sidings can be led from the reversing loop.

Extendable layouts

A model railway layout, even a small one, will take some time to build. Indeed, as much of the pleasure of railway modelling is in the construction work we would not want to complete the layout too soon. However, it is nice to be able to alternate building and operating as the mood takes us. Ideally we need a layout which begins small, so that we can get something running on it as soon as possible, but which can be extended in stages thus maintaining its interest. In this way there will be a period of track laying and wiring to reach the next stage, followed by a

The point-to-point design is easily extended by adding one or more further sections between the original units.

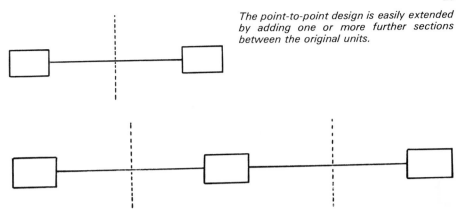

pause to build structures and scenery and perhaps more rolling stock. You can also enjoy operating the extended layout. The layout should be arranged so that it is fully usable at each stage. Thus there will be no need to go on to the next stage until you feel you want to.

The point-to-point type of layout, for example a branch line of the terminus to fiddle yard design, is very easily extended particularly if the terminus and fiddle yard are on separate baseboard sections. All that is needed is to add extra sections between the two original units. At every stage the layout will be fully operational and further sections can be completed at your leisure. Such a system can be very versatile. You can, for example, remove a section you no longer want and replace it with another more interesting one, or you can take one unit out for rebuilding and still run the layout in the meantime. If you want you can even arrange the sections so that they will fit together in more than one order to give extra variety to the operation of the layout. While the additional sections for a point-to-point line will probably be narrow units carrying a single line there is no reason why an oval or spiral should not be included if it suits the space available and you want it.

Many enthusiasts start with an oval track plan, often developed from the train set. The simple oval needs a passing track and a few sidings to make it sufficiently interesting to operate. For the next stage of the layout one of the sidings on the outside of the oval can be extended to form a branch line. This can be carried away from the main oval on an extension of the baseboard or it can be kept on the original base but raised up to a higher level. Alternatively the main oval can be

elevated so that the branch can lead down to a reversing loop beneath it.

Another development of the oval is to raise part of it so that it crosses over the level section to result in a spiral point-to-point scheme. There are many possible ways in which the simple oval can be added to and modified particularly if the so called 'cookie cutter' method of baseboard construction is employed. In this system a simple grid frame is used to support a baseboard top of plywood which is fixed on to the frame with screws only. The tracks are then laid and the railway is used until the modeller wants to develop it further. To raise the level of a track saw cuts are made with a keyhole or sabre saw along each side of the track, taking care not to cut the frame beneath the plywood. Any screws holding this strip down are removed and, the strip and the track it supports, are elevated to the required height. Wooden riser blocks are fitted to hold it in its new position.

It is helpful when planning to extend a layout in this way if you have some idea at the beginning how you will want to do this later. You can then put sidings on the original layout at points where branch lines or other tracks will leave the oval later. Thus the points needed will already be in place avoiding the job of taking up part of the track and fitting points in later.

One of the benefits in building up your layout in stages is that you do not need to decide on the details of these later stages until you actually start work on them. Thus the experience you gain from the first part of the layout will influence the form which the extensions will take, and the finished layout will be more likely to meet your eventual requirements.

Track schemes

The oval can be developed by adding branches inside or outside.

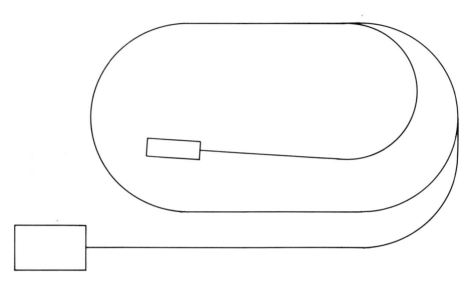

Here two branches have been added but the design is not a good one as a train proceeding from one terminus must reverse, at some stage after reaching the oval, to get onto the other branch.

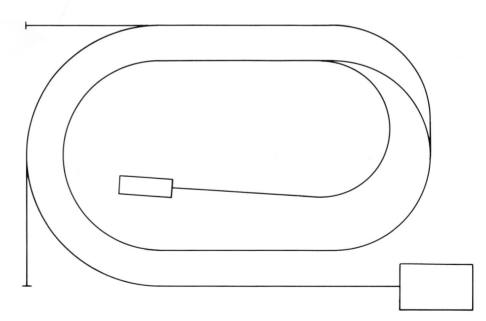

This is the better design and allows interesting operation combining, as it does, a continuous run on the oval with point-to-point operation on the branches.

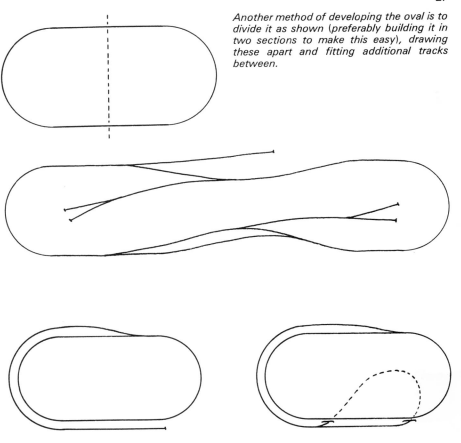

Another method of developing the oval is to divide it as shown (preferably building it in two sections to make this easy), drawing these apart and fitting additional tracks between.

Here the original oval has been elevated so that the branch can go to a reversing loop situated beneath the oval.

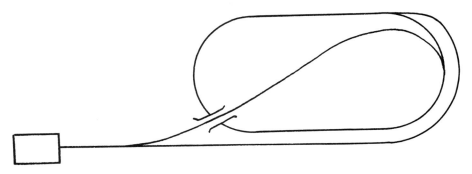

This oval with a single branch has a reversing loop incorporated so that trains can run out and back from the terminus and do as many laps as desired round the oval.

Track schemes

Railway types

On a model railway layout it is quite imposs- ible to include everything and compromise and selection are essential. Obviously it is best to concentrate on the parts of the prototype which interest you most. If your interests are rather varied there is nothing to stop you mixing prototypes and periods on one layout, if you wish, but your model railway is more likely to be satisfying to view and operate if it is more realistic and authentic. The highly accurate and detailed models now available commercially will also look at their best in a proper setting.

Your modelling will benefit from know- ledge of the real thing, either from direct observation of the prototype or from the study of photographs, drawings, railway and model railway magazines and books. Though basing your model on the prototype will help realism it is not generally possible, or even desirable, to try to copy part of a real railway exactly. Instead, select the features which you find the most characteristic and appealing, and leave out those you feel are unnecessary or undesirable, so creating your own ideal representation of the prototype.

There are various types of railways depending on the location, circumstances and type of traffic. We can model our layout on any of these and the following listing gives some idea of the possibilities. There is often some overlap between the different cate- gories; it may also be possible to include more than one type of railway on a layout.

Main line

The main lines with their fast long trains are a very interesting and exciting part of the real railways and there is an excellent selection of suitable model locomotives and rolling stock now available, making a main line a tempting choice. However, to do the prototype justice a large layout with a good length of run, large radius curves, double track and platforms able to accommodate long trains is really desirable. A main line 00-scale layout can be built in a small space but this involves

considerable compromise. Train lengths of only 4 or 5 coaches and curves of 18 or even 15 in radius may be required. However, some imagination must be used with any model railway layout, and you may be prepared to stretch it further if you are really set on the idea of a main line layout. A convenient arrangement is a continuous run scheme, either a simple oval or a twice around or figure of eight design so that length of run can be achieved by letting the train make a number of laps of the circuit.

Though I am hesitant to recommend it to the beginner for a first effort, because of its greater extent and the need for a lifting section at the door, a layout around the walls of a room is an ideal arrangement if you are sure you want a main line model. If you have a suitable site and you wish to tackle a layout of this type, start very simply with just a single track circuit. Planning in advance where points will be needed later is helpful as they can then be included in the correct positions in the basic circuit as you lay it. In this way you will avoid the need to remove sections of track later to fit the points in. In due course you can install a second circuit to make the line double track. Station tracks, goods yards, an engine depot, sidings and so on can all be added in stages as time and money are available.

An alternative to the continuous run layout is an L-shaped terminus to fiddle yard scheme of the type developed for branch line models, but with the station adapted for main line practice, though again with restricted train lengths. If the layout is fitted into the corner of a room, it could later be extended, if circumstances permit, by introducing new sections between the station and the fiddle yard. Eventually it could be carried right round the room to form a complete circuit, with the station converted from a terminus into a through type.

In N scale a 180° turn can be made on a 2 ft wide board and this makes it possible to model a main line through station on a

The main station on Graham Bailey's modern period British Rail N-scale layout uses parts from three Pola kits for the glass roof while the remainder of the station was scratch-built.

narrow board along one wall, or curved to fit onto an L-shaped baseboard along two walls, with the baseboard widening to 2 ft at each end to accommodate loops to provide continuous running. The loops can be hidden by scenery to conceal their sharp radii and also the fact that the trains go round and round on the layout. If it is important to keep the layout as narrow as possible throughout, 9 in radius Peco Setrack sectional track can be used for the loops and the turn can be made on a baseboard only 20 in wide.

If the modeller merely enjoys seeing his trains run in a realistic setting, but is not concerned about operation, a very simple diorama type of layout can be constructed in N scale which can be fitted along one wall as a shelf. A dog bone track design will produce what appears to be double track main line while the loops at each end, allowing continuous running, can be concealed. The scenic work should be carried out carefully to give a realistic effect. The landscape can rise at the rear of the layout to cover hidden sidings holding other trains.

Branch line

If we want to achieve a model railway as realistic as possible within the restrictions imposed by a small layout we must look for a suitable prototype and the country branch line in the days of steam is an ideal choice. Trains often consisted of only two or three coaches pulled by a small tank engine and the station track layouts were usually fairly simple. An attractive branch line type of layout can easily be developed from the train set oval and can be an ideal first permanent layout with considerable scope for attractive scenery and structures.

During the 1950s the branch line model railway layout concept was developed considerably. The idea was not so much to provide a suitable subject for beginners as to enable more experienced modellers to create a model railway which would look and operate realistically in a small space. The short prototype trains allowed the modeller to run authentic length trains despite the small size of his layout. Also because the station track layouts are simple on branch lines they can be compressed to fit onto a model railway while still retaining their essential features, so that the model can be operated according to prototype practice and following a proper timetable. Rather than copy any particular station exactly, the modeller will usually do better to select desirable features from various prototypes to produce an interesting and attractive station.

Railway types

Because the aim was realistic operation, the point-to-point track arrangement was preferred to the continuous run schemes and the now classic branch line terminus to fiddle yard (hidden sidings representing the rest of the system) design was developed. Such a track plan can be fitted onto baseboards of various shapes but a popular arrangement is on two narrow baseboards in an L-shape, often fitted into the corner of a room. This

A branch line terminus modelled in 00 scale. The layout is operated as a point-to-point line with a fiddle yard at the other end.

design has the advantage of providing the greatest running possibilities in a minimum area and often a layout of this shape can be fitted into a room whereas a conventional rectangular baseboard would not be accept-

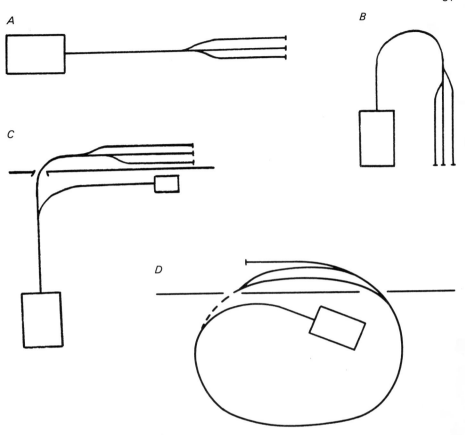

Branch Lines. The basic branch line terminus to fiddle yard design (a). This can be bent to a U-shape if desired (b). An L-shaped terminus to fiddle yard scheme with an additional station, dock, factory or other feature in front of the fiddle yard and separated from it by a backscene (c). The Maurice Deane terminus to fiddle yard design with a backscene separating the two (d). Note the optional link track (dotted) providing a continuous run if required.

able as it would block the centre of the room too much.

A branch line layout of this type is also very suitable for the beginner as it can fairly quickly be brought to a stage where it is interesting to view and operate. However, the scope is limited and in time the modeller will wish to extend the layout. This is another reason for not basing the model accurately on a specific prototype because if you do, once you have completed the model no further development is possible. If, however, your layout is merely based in general terms on the practice of the prototype you have chosen, you are free to alter or add to your model indefinitely.

An interesting alternative to the usual scheme, first employed, I believe, by Maurice Deane, is to fit the branch line on a rectangular baseboard with the fiddle yard behind the terminus but concealed by a low backscene. This has two advantages. The modeller can easily reach both the terminus and the fiddle yard from his operating position in the central well. It also makes it easy to include a link to allow continuous running for locomotives to be run in or when the modeller would like to just sit back and watch the trains in action. The link can be concealed so that the realism of the point-to-point scheme is not impaired.

The branch line provides the opportunity for realistic operation and also has great scenic possibilities. GWR branches are

Railway types

As the mainline will probably be chosen to model, some compromise will be needed on a small layout but there are some advantages to modern image modelling compared to a mainline layout in steam days. In many cases the trains are now shorter and many tracks have been lifted simplifying track layouts and goods yards. Engine servicing facilities are also much simpler with diesel fuel tanks replacing coal and water and with no need for turntables. The modeller can introduce some modern architecture in addition to the older buildings still in use giving an interesting variety. Overhead catenary is also very effective in model form and a working catenary can be assembled from parts made by Vollmer or Sommerfeldt. In this case two trains can be controlled independently on the same stretch of track, one from the track as usual and one from the overhead.

One of the great advantages of modelling modern railways is that one can still study the real thing easily to gain information on anything from locomotives down to small details such as signs and noticeboards. On the goods side a Freightliner depot would make an interesting working model. As modern trains are often run as block units

The Market Redwing GWR branch layout is a portable one which has been exhibited on several occasions. At shows the railway is operated on an hourly programme and the card system illustrated here indicates to the spectators what the next train movement will be. As each operation is completed the next card is turned down.

particularly popular and are very well catered for with commercial models, but other prototypes can also be followed very satisfactorily if preferred.

Modern image

There is considerable interest in modelling present day British Rail, particularly among younger enthusiasts. The locomotive and rolling stock requirements are generally well catered for by the trade with even the High Speed Train available, as a ready-to-run model in 00 and as a kit in N scale. There is a reasonable range of diesels and a few electrics with further models planned in the ready-to-run category and there is also a selection of diesels and multiple units in kit form, particularly from MTK and Q kits which helps to complete the motive power scene. There is also a good variety of rolling stock suitable for a modern layout.

The attractive Hornby 00-scale model of the British Rail High Speed Train seen on the exhibition layout of the Bournemouth & Isle of Purbeck MRC. Note the non-operating model of a miniature railway on the promenade below the station and the beach at lower right.

Mike Sharman has constructed a fine Victorian period 4 mm scale layout which features standard-, narrow- and broad-gauge track together with some complex multiple gauge trackwork. Careful research and accurate modelling, mostly from scratch, has recreated the atmosphere of the railways of that period very effectively. Locomotive No 10 is a model of Timothy Hackworth's 0-6-0 built in 1838 for the Stockton & Darlington Railway and is the oldest prototype represented on the layout. The working beam engine behind No 10 was also scratch-built.

there is rather less opportunity for train marshalling and shunting on a modern layout, but we can still install some industrial sidings for local shunting.

Period

Though strictly the term refers to any era, including the present, I use it here to mean historical, for any time prior to the contemporary scene. Construction of an historical layout requires research and also care to avoid introducing anachronisms. Depending on the period chosen the modeller may also have to build more or less all his locomotives and rolling stock himself.

The most popular period seems to be the pre-nationalisation era, particularly of the 1930s, and of the four main railway companies, the LMS, the LNER, the SR and the GWR, the greatest following is for the GWR, with especial interest in its branchlines. There is now a good selection of ready-to-run models and kits enabling the modeller to construct a successful model of this type.

A period which has many advantages but which is not yet particularly popular is the post-nationalisation era of the 1950s. A layout based on this period can mix an interesting variety of steam, diesel and electric locomotives and of rolling stock. The modeller is well served with commercial models and there is no problem in obtaining information and photographs.

At the other end of the time scale are the early Victorian railways. The modeller who chooses these as his prototype will need to carry out considerable research and there is little available commercially to help him in construction. However, if well executed such a layout can be most interesting and attractive. Mike Sharman has built a superb 4 mm scale layout of this period; careful research and skilled scratch-building has created an authentic atmosphere as can be seen in the above photograph.

Going back to even earlier times, 1825-30, the American MRC of Darlington chose the Stockton & Darlington Railway as their prototype and built a fascinating model of great historical interest for the Rail 150 exhibition in 1975. The scale was also 4 mm.

Railway types

A view of W. T. Butler's Dalcross layout, a 4 mm scale model of a 19th century ironworks. The accurate modelling of an unusual prototype and the inclusion of many small, but authentic details, has resulted in a fascinating model. The locomotives, rolling stock, structures and steam lorries were all hand-built.

Industrial

The industrial railway layout has considerable potential in a small space as it can be essentially a shunting layout and need not have an oval or other form of continuous run, though one can be included if desired and if there is sufficient space. In its simplest form the track plan need only have a run-around loop and a number of sidings though the addition of hidden sidings or a fiddle yard, concealed by structures, low relief buildings or a backscene, will add to the operating potential. For a long, narrow layout the switchback type of track plan is useful for an industrial line, while if a rectangular baseboard can be used an oval with sidings can be a convenient track arrangement.

As the locomotives will be small steam or diesel engines and the rolling stock mainly goods vehicles, the layout can have sharp

There are many prototype industries which can be adapted to make interesting features for model railway layouts. This small scrap yard in 4 mm scale was based on a yard in Newcastle but was considerably compressed to suit the space available on a layout.

curves. If the modeller wishes he can include some interesting trackwork as the prototype is often cramped and needs slips, 3-way or lap points, curved points and crossings. The track is often set into roads or wharves so that road vehicles can cross the tracks easily and this should also be represented on the model.

There is a good selection of suitable small locomotives in ready-to-run and kit form. Centre Models have specialised in industrial steam locomotives, offering cast metal kits for four different types in 00 scale, and some of the smaller engines made by other cast metal kit manufacturers are also ideal for a layout of this type. A wide range of suitable rolling stock both ready-to-run and in kit form is on the market.

The layout can be based on one major industry such as a mine and processing plant, a large factory or a shipyard, or can represent an industrial area or estate with a variety of different types of industries giving scope for a wide range of rolling stock. A dock or canal is often very attractive in model form.

The small size of N scale makes it possible to represent the larger industries more realistically than is usually possible in 00 scale. Graham Bailey modelled this shipbuilding yard for his N-scale British Rail layout using a modified Novo Shell Welder kit as the ship under construction.

An industrial layout also offers excellent opportunities for structure modelling and detailing. Because the prototype is often cramped, with tracks winding between numerous buildings we can fit a great deal into a small area on a layout without loss of realism. There are a number of fine kits for industrial structures on the market, mainly plastic kits manufactured on the Continent. These can be modified and combined to produce even greater variety or the modeller can scratch-build his structures, perhaps following actual prototypes. Several working models are also available as kits including a dock crane, a gantry crane, an aerial ropeway, gravel loaders and a conveyor belt, and these will add extra activity and interest to the layout. The possibilities for detailing an industrial model railway layout are almost limitless and the modeller might like to illuminate the buildings, perhaps employing fibre optics.

If the opportunity arises to build a larger layout eventually the industrial layout can be incorporated into it forming a factory area which can generate much interesting traffic and shunting activity.

Narrow gauge

Not only are the narrow-gauge prototypes very attractive and appealing but they also have many other features which make them ideal subjects for modelling. The short trains, small locomotives and rolling stock, sharp curves, steep gradients and simple station track plans are all useful to the enthusiast trying to fit a model railway into a small space.

The modeller may choose to base his layout on one of the preserved lines, either as it is today or as it was in its earlier days. There are a number of locomotive and rolling stock kits now available, mainly in 009, for British prototypes which will assist the modeller in a project of this sort but he will also need to do some converting and scratch-building to complete the roster. Obviously if the modeller chooses to represent the line as it is today there will be no problem in gaining accurate information about the railway and its stock. There is also a good deal of data available about the better known railways in their earlier days so it should not be too difficult to make an authentic model.

Alternatively, the enthusiast may prefer to model an imaginery line thus giving him more scope for introducing features he finds interesting or attractive. He may base his model in a general way on one prototype or perhaps on aspects of several.

Railway types

The Vale of Tallynog is a model of a small Welsh narrow-gauge railway constructed by Phil Savage, a member of the Wessex 009 Society. The fiddle yard can be seen behind the retaining wall. The excellent detailing of the railway terminus and dock gives the layout a very realistic appearance.

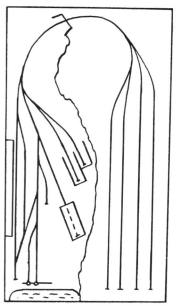

Track plan for Phil Savage's 009 Vale of Tallynog layout, a U-shaped terminus to fiddle yard design. (Plan not to scale.)

Many of the overseas narrow-gauge lines are also very appealing and with the selection of ready-to-run models, particularly Swiss and Austrian prototypes, in HO9 a layout can be built without difficulty. For realism, the modeller should try to create the atmosphere of the original by studying book or magazine pictures and perhaps by visiting the real thing on holiday. The track arrangements differ from those typical of British practice and the model should be based on actual track plans if possible. While the availability of ready-to-run equipment and the greater familiarity of European prototypes tempts modellers to choose these there are many attractive narrow-gauge railways in other parts of the world which could also make excellent layouts. An example is Howard Coulson's 'Eitomo' layout in 009 based on East African prototypes. Study of the real thing from books and magazines together with good scenic work has enabled Howard to capture the atmosphere of these lines very effectively. Most of his locomotives and rolling stock are conversions of commercially available 009 or N-scale models and are closely based on East African prototypes.

Many American narrow-gauge modellers work in HOn3, HO-scale models of 3 ft gauge

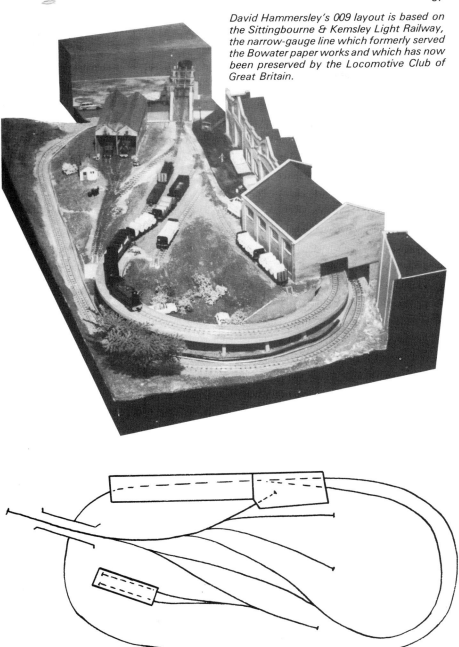

Track plan of the 009 layout built by David Hammersley and based on the Bowater Railway. The track design is an oval, partly concealed by structures, with a branch rising from it to the higher central part of the layout. (Plan is not to scale.)

Railway types

Howard Coulson has based his 009 narrow-gauge 'Eitomo' layout on East African prototype lines. With careful research and imaginative modelling he has given his layout the atmosphere of the real thing. The locomotives (including the Climax shown here) and rolling stock are mostly conversions of commercial 009- and N-scale products.

prototypes, but some are using 9 mm gauge to model lines such as the Maine 2 ft gauge railways in HO scale, and this would be a more convenient choice for modellers in Britain as there are more commercial items available for conversion.

The introduction of ready-to-run models in 009 led to the development of the so-called 'rabbit' layouts. Modellers took advantage of the sharp curves and steep gradients possible in this scale to pack a great deal of track at various levels onto a very small baseboard, with mountainous scenery and with trains popping in and out of tunnels like rabbits in and out of burrows. Realism is of course compromised but the layouts are very entertaining to build and operate. With good scenery they are very attractive and make an ideal coffee table or display layout for the lounge.

An alternative to an entire layout in narrow gauge is the addition of a narrow-gauge feeder to a standard-gauge layout. This is an ideal arrangement as it gives you a chance to see how you like narrow-gauge modelling without committing yourself to more than a short length of track to start with. If you like it you can then extend the narrow-gauge section. I should perhaps warn you that there is a tendency for it to take over at the expense of the standard gauge! A narrow-gauge line will add interest and extra activity to the

layout using only space which would not be of much use for standard-gauge tracks.

Combining standard and narrow gauge on the layout gives the opportunity for including interesting dual-gauge trackwork. However, with the exception of a dual 16.5 mm/9 mm gauge crossing made by Liliput, you will have to build any dual-gauge track yourself, a task for the more experienced modeller.

Liliput make this crossing for 00 gauge (16.5 mm) and 009 (9 mm) which may be useful when combining a standard- and narrow-gauge line on a layout.

Foreign

I have made some mention of modelling foreign railways in the section on narrow gauge and similar principles apply to standard gauge with regard to familiarising yourself with everything about the prototype and its setting if you hope to create a realistic

This 009 narrow-gauge layout owned by the Poole & District Model Railway Society measures only 36 in × 27 in but includes a track run of over 12 ft, two sidings, two stations and many interesting scenic features! It is an example of the so-called rabbit layout.

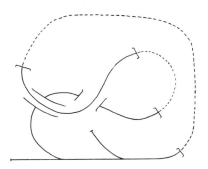

The Poole & District MRS 009 layout is a simple 'rabbit' type with a dog bone design where one loop partly overlaps the other. Two sidings add extra interest. (Plan not to scale.)

model. Operating practice and track layout is often rather different from the British system and this should be taken into account when designing a layout.

For US modelling the range of ready-to-run models, kits and parts in HO and N scales is excellent and the enthusiast can obtain a great deal of information about modelling American railroads from reading one or more of the excellent model railroad magazines produced in the States.

The range of European models in HO and N scales is also very good though the emphasis is almost entirely on ready-to-run equipment; this is generally of excellent quality. Some countries, particularly Germany, France and Switzerland, are very well catered for by the manufacturers but for others there is much less available. There is a good deal of prototype information, in England, for the modeller and several countries have model railway magazines, though here there may be language problems of course. Ideally one should visit the country concerned and take as many photographs as possible to guide you in modelling the setting, the trackside details and so on.

For other countries of the world much converting or scratch-building will be required to complete a layout and such a project is only suitable for the more experienced modeller with a particular interest in and knowledge of the railway system concerned.

Preserved line

I briefly mentioned the possibility of modelling a preserved line in the narrow-gauge section. For the modeller who likes, and has perhaps already collected, a wide variety of locomotives which would not normally be seen together because of their origins, period or type, a very attractive solution can be a preserved standard-gauge line. One could even include some foreign

Railway types

A scene on a typical US branchline modelled in HO scale. The beautifully detailed corrugated iron warehouse was built from a Campbell's kit. (Photograph by courtesy of Leo Campbell.)

Jouef offer a wide selection of French prototype models in HO scale including this interesting train of double-decker commuter coaches seen here on the Hestair Models' exhibition layout.

engines if desired as there are several prototype precedents for this!

The modeller might like to base his layout on an actual preserved line. This has the advantage that he can visit the railway to see and photograph everything and there is often plenty of published data about the locomotives, rolling stock and so on. The model could be a representation of the line as it is, or as the preservation society hope to make it. Such a model could be very satisfying and could also have considerable publicity value for the railway. Providing locomotives and stock for most lines should not be a problem using the standard commercial products.

Another approach would be to model a branch line you like and which has been closed, as though it had been preserved. This will give you more freedom in the design of the layout and in the choice of locomotives

and rolling stock than if you were modelling an actual preserved line. A third alternative is to model an entirely imaginary preserved line of your own design.

There are many interesting details which could be added to a layout of this type. There may be locomotives and stock awaiting or undergoing repair, some scrapped items kept to provide spare parts for other stock, many parts lying around, and numerous visitors, some with cameras taking pictures. There could also be a small museum of other items such as traction engines, vintage cars or buses, and so on.

If you model a station on the preserved line as one combined with British Rail then you have the perfect excuse for including everything from vintage steam engines on the preserved line to the High Speed Train on the BR tracks! All on the one layout!

The working traverser on Mike Sharman's period layout with its nicely detailed vertical boilered donkey engine. The locomotive is 'Pegasus' a 2-4-0 built in 1870 by Joseph Beattie for the London & South Western Railway. Locomotive and traverser were both hand-built.

Railway types

More specialised railway types

Engine depot

One approach to modelling on a small layout is to choose a prototype line which can be compressed without losing its essential features, the branch line being a good example. Another method can be to select a small part of a larger prototype system and model only that section. As many modellers buy or build more and larger locomotives than can reasonably be accommodated on the usual small layout, an apt choice can be to model a motive power depot. Such a model need occupy only a small area but will be ideal as a setting for displaying and operating locomotive models. If hidden sidings are included the layout could even be

Part of the garden railway layout built by Dave Howsam and Ron Prattley. Figures, plants and garden fittings are Britains' models. (Photo by Ron Prattley.)

operated to a timetable, with locomotives leaving the shed, taking on coal and water and proceeding to their duties. Later they will return from the hidden sidings to be prepared for the next day's work.

Though such a layout is unusual it could be interesting to build, with plenty of opportunities for super-detailing interesting structures and, if desired, a turntable. A crane and a snowplough are among the items of unusual rolling stock which can be stored on sidings on the layout. Extra details could include a hoist and perhaps an engine undergoing repairs, or one which has been scrapped. The scope of the model can be increased by providing facilities for diesels as well.

A layout of this type could be ideal for the modeller who is a club member and can enjoy more conventional operating on the club layout but wants somewhere to display his locomotives. It is also a useful unit for the modeller who has no space for a layout at present but is building up a collection of locomotive models for the time when he will be able to construct a layout. The engine depot will allow him to enjoy some construction work, provide a setting for his engines and can be incorporated into a layout later.

Military railways

From the American Civil War right through to the Second World War, railways have played an important military role. With the great popularity of both railway and military modelling I am sure that many enthusiasts are interested in both and I am surprised that so few military railway layouts have been built. The ideal prototype would perhaps be the extensive narrow-gauge railway system which operated in France during the First World War tanks, soldiers and horse-drawn *First World War* by W.J.K. Davies (David & Charles) covers this subject in detail, even including dimensioned drawings of the locomotives and rolling stock. In 009 the equipment could be represented well with commercially available items, modified in some cases. Such a layout could be built in a small space and the scenic work could be very effective, with ruined buildings, First World War tanks, soldiers and horse drawn equipment, trenches, look-out posts and so on. The Airfix 00-scale military models would be especially useful in this detailing.

Some of the most interesting and impressive pieces of military railway equipment are the railway guns, and the enthusiast may well like to include several of these models on his layout. One approach might be to construct an industrial railway layout based on a factory producing these guns. Such a model would permit shunting and also act as an effective setting for displaying the model rail guns.

A different type of military railway layout would be one based on one of the military railways operated in Britain. The Longmoor Military Railway used for training army personnel in railway operating has been well documented and could make an interesting model. The Royal Aircraft Establishment railway at Farnborough would make an unusual variant on the industrial railway theme. The major traffic here is coal brought in by rail to the power station, but wood and steel sections are also transported.

Rack railways

Mountain railways may be fitted with a rack in the centre of the track with which a driven gear on the locomotives meshes thus ensuring good traction and no slipping. The only British prototype is the Snowdon Mountain Railway.

In model form Fleischmann provide locomotives and track, but no points, for both HO and N scales. The lack of points mean that only a simple single track line can be constructed unless the modeller is prepared to make points himself. However, a rack railway can be an attractive addition to a conventional layout, providing extra activity and an excuse for some mountainous scenery.

Underground railways

Underground railways have been rather neglected by modellers though there does seem to have been more interest recently with the appearance of a few layouts including models of London Transport tube trains, one built by an enthusiast in Holland! An LT layout would make an interesting model. Much of the track should be modelled on parts of the system above ground with only part of it in tunnels. Alternatively, an underground model could be added to an ordinary urban or suburban area layout, in which case it might be best to keep it entirely beneath ground level so that it does not take up space which could be used for the rest of the layout.

Garden railway

Dave Howsam and Ron Prattley produced a most unusual but attractive model some years ago of a garden in 10 mm to the foot scale using Britains' figures and garden fittings with N-scale model locomotives,

More specialised railway types

The relatively small size of N-scale models has enabled Graham Bailey to provide comprehensive steam and diesel locomotive servicing facilities on his moderate sized British Rail layout. These include a steam locomotive roundhouse (above left), coaling stage (above), diesel engine house (left), diesel fuelling depot (below left) and a train washing unit (below).

A model tramway system can be an interesting addition to a model railway layout. The two views above and right are of Adrian Swain's 00-scale tramway. British tram models are available in 00 and N scales as cast metal kits; Continental prototype models are manufactured as ready-to-run items in HO and N scales.

rolling stock and track representing a 10¼ in gauge garden railway. The track layout on this model was very simple so operating scope was limited but the layout was intended especially for display and was very successful. There is no reason why a more extensive system could not be modelled in this way. A miniature railway, though not of course in the garden, which would make a very interesting prototype for a project of this sort is the well known Ravenglass & Eskdale Railway.

Monorails

These make intriguing models but do call for

scratch-building by the modeller. Though model monorails are rather rare, the Listowel & Ballybunion (an early Irish monorail) seems to be an appealing prototype, perhaps because it is so unusual. I know of models of this line in various scales by no fewer than five modellers; the largest of these models are the superb 16 mm scale locomotives made by Don Boreham and Adrian Garner.

Trams

Trams are not strictly railway models in the usual sense, though a tramway layout can be very appealing. The sharp curves and short 'trains' (for British prototypes usually a single

tramcar, though European trams often pull trailers) enable an interesting layout to be built in a small area. As the setting will probably be an urban one the possibilities for structure modelling and detailing are considerable. A tram system can also be added to a model railway layout and will increase the action on the layout, even with a very simple tram system.

Ready-to-run European tram models are available in HO and N scales while British cast metal kits are made in 00 and N scales. A few HO-scale German prototype cast metal tram

kits are also produced.

Most modellers will want to build a conventional type of layout, the branch line and industrial railway being particularly suitable for the beginner. However, I feel it is worth while to indicate, as I have above, that the possible scope in the hobby is much wider than that; it is always worth while considering something a little different for your modelling, provided it is a subject which appeals to you and in which you are sufficiently interested to do any research which is necessary.

More specialised railway types

Track planning

00 scale

Having looked at the basic track schemes and considered the various types of railways that can be modelled we have reached the stage of planning the track arrangement for a layout. The usual method is to draw to scale the outline of the layout baseboard and then to plot in the tracks on this plan. A convenient scale is 1 in to the foot or, for small layouts, even 2 in to the foot. Unfortunately many plans are not drawn properly, either through lack of care or due to a desire to squeeze that little bit more into the layout. The errors particularly relate to points, for which inadequate allowance is made for lengths and radii, and to clearances which are insufficient. It is very important to draw everything accurately to scale as errors here will cause problems later when you try to construct the layout. Though a neatly drawn out plan (complete with attractive scenic details sketched in) looks very nice it is by no means necessary for this planning work. A roughly drawn plan is perfectly adequate provided the modeller keeps accurately to scale measurements.

Tracks should be arranged so that the centre lines are not less than 1½ in from the baseboard edge and a greater clearance is better if it is possible. The track centres for 2 tracks running parallel should be 2 in apart. The curve radius chosen as the minimum will depend on the type of equipment that will be run on the layout, on the space available and on the type of railway modelled. The usual minimum for proprietary models is 15 in radius, but 18 or 24 in curves are desirable, and curves of larger radius still will look better if they can be accommodated. When plotting the track positions we must start a curve at a point a distance at least equal to the radius of the curve plus the clearance needed, from the end of the layout. If the curve can be started further back we can either use a larger radius curve or allow more clearance. As the curve is often one of 180° at the end of the layout we must also check on the width,

which will be twice the sum of the radius and the clearance, in relation to the baseboard width. The appearance of small radius curves can be improved considerably by fitting a curve of twice the radius between the straight and the true curve as a transitional section. This will require more space than the simple minimum radius curve, of course, and suitable allowance must be made if you wish to do this.

Points are more difficult to draw to scale and care should be taken to allow sufficient space for them. You should measure the points you intend to use and use this length as a guide, preferably allowing a little extra to give you some leeway in case of any slight errors during track laying. For example, I allow 7 in for Hornby, 8 in for Peco 2 ft radius, and 9 in for Peco 3 ft radius points, and 8 in for a Peco crossing. I want to stress that you should stick closely to the measurements for points and crossings and resist any temptation to cut things finer. These parts cannot be altered so if you have not allowed the right amount of space your layout will not be correct — other parts being distorted with detrimental effects.

A fairly commonly employed track arrangement is a reversing loop. This requires a distance of three times the radius of the curves for the loop itself, together with another radius on the end to join with the other tracks. The width of the loop is twice the radius. Clearances must be added to these figures.

If one track is to pass over another a clearance of at least 2½ in and preferably 3 in is required. As the maximum gradient that should be used is 1 in 30 a distance of 90 in, 7 ft 6 in, is needed to clear the low level track if only one track is on a gradient. If one track rises and the other falls, both at 1 in 30, the distance is halved to 45 in, 3 ft 9 in respectively. These figures assume the more desirable minimum of 3 in clearance is adopted. If the track is curved we need to

Diagram A

Diagram B

Track planning in 00 scale *Many modellers when drawing out a scale plan make the points too short and give them too wide an angle; this causes problems when you try to construct the layout as the points will not fit into the space allowed.*

If we draw in the centre lines for the straight and diverging tracks on a pair of points as in Diagram A we can see there is a point at which these lines meet and that they meet at an angle. To draw points accurately on our track plans we need to locate the point at which the lines meet correctly and to draw the true angle from it.

We can do this as in Diagram B, using the dimensions given in the table for 'A' and 'B', and we can then be confident that the plan will be accurate with respect to the points.

Point radius	'A'	'B'
18 inch	*2½ inch*	*3½ units*
24 inch	*3 inch*	*4 units*
36 inch	*3½ inch*	*5 units*

These dimensions are easily obtained by measuring directly the points you intend to use and you can make your own listing to suit your choice of points.

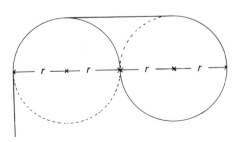

The reversing loop together with a lead out is equivalent in space to two circles side by side and the length required is therefore at least four times the minimum radius.

know its length for working out the gradient. As the circumference of a circle is given by $2\pi r$ we will be close enough if we call π 3 and reckon the circumference as 6 times the radius. That is in every ¼ circle the track distance is 1½ times the radius. For 18 in radius curves therefore, the distance for a quarter circle is 27 in.

Station platforms will be 4½-5 in wide and the platform edge should be an inch from the track centre line. Platform lengths depend on the train lengths and a convenient estimate is to allow 1 ft per coach. If platforms must be short, model a small station and keep train lengths down also. Stations are usually modelled with straight platforms but the introduction of a slight curve can be attractive.

A terminus station will need a run-around loop so that the engine can be moved to the other end of the train for the return journey. The loop can either go alongside the platform or can be on the line beyond the platform so it may also be used for goods trains. The loop must, of course, be long enough to hold the trains and there must also be sufficient room on the track beyond it for the locomotive, say 8 in for a tank engine and as much as 12 in for a tender locomotive.

Goods facilities can be very simple, merely a siding or two entered by trailing points, or there may be a larger yard with a headshunt, so that shunting can take place without blocking the main line. A run-around loop may be provided but often the passenger loop can be shared. When planning sidings and passing loops try to avoid reverse or 'S' curves.

Kick-back sidings are sometimes included on a model railway layout. Access to one of these is only possible if the siding from which it leads is empty already or is cleared at the time. Because of this the modeller may find that he does not use the kick-back siding as he does not want to be bothered with carrying out the extra moves required. Conversely, however, we can take the view that anything which involves more shunting movements adds to the operating activity and makes the layout more interesting. It is a matter of personal choice whether you want to keep operation simple and easy or to make it as complex as you can. Modellers who particularly enjoy operation and shunting may choose to model an industrial line on which numerous complications such as kick-back sidings, several industries being served by one siding making access more difficult, and so on, can be introduced.

Engine servicing facilities may also be very

Track planning

Some examples of station plans—not to scale.

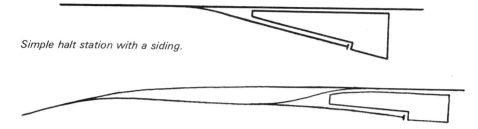

Simple halt station with a siding.

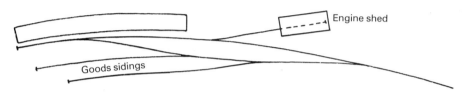

Simple through station with run around loop so trains from either direction can shunt the siding and so trains can be reversed. The loop can also double up as a siding.

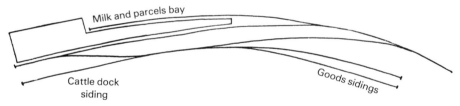

Small terminus station with run-around loop, goods sidings and engine shed.

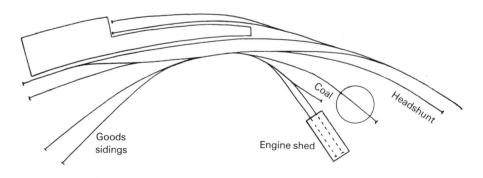

Slightly larger terminus station with parcels, milk and cattle dock sidings but no engine shed.

Larger terminus station with more comprehensive engine servicing facilities including a turntable so tender locomotives can be turned. A headshunt has been provided so shunting can be carried out without blocking the main line.

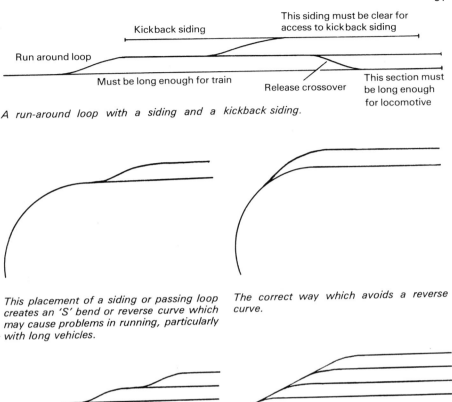

A run-around loop with a siding and a kickback siding.

This placement of a siding or passing loop creates an 'S' bend or reverse curve which may cause problems in running, particularly with long vehicles.

The correct way which avoids a reverse curve.

This arrangement of sidings creates a whole series of reverse curves and also wastes space.

The correct design for a series of sidings.

simple, merely a single track engine shed with coaling stage, water tower and ash pit for one engine at a branch line terminus, or a larger depot may be modelled with a 2 or 3 track shed and perhaps a turntable for tender locomotives. If a point-to-point system has a turntable at one terminus there should also be one at the other terminus (except, of course, if it is a fiddle yard) so that engines can always run facing the correct way. A turntable is quite a large feature so you should consider carefully before including one if you are short of space. A 9 in diameter table will accommodate small engines but larger locomotives will need an 11 in table.

It is essential to provide proper access to track, points and rolling stock; check your own easy reach at the height you intend to have your layout and use this as a guide when planning the layout. If you want to have a

central operating well do not make this too small; 4 ft × 2ft is a reasonable minimum. Make sure that access to tunnels will also be easy.

For the actual drawing out only fairly simple drawing instruments are needed; a sharp pencil, a pair of compasses, a set square, a ruler and an eraser are the essentials. Templates, for the curves you will be using in the scale of your drawing, can be cut from card or, even better, transparent plastic, and will be very useful. Many modellers work on white card rather than on paper when drawing up layout plans as frequent alterations can be made without crumpling the material or spoiling the surface.

While it is very convenient to draw out plans to 1 or 2 in to the foot scale in the early stages, there is much to be said for drawing

Track planning

Small motive power depots.

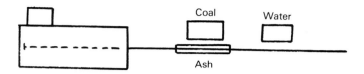

Very simple engine facilities for a small station.

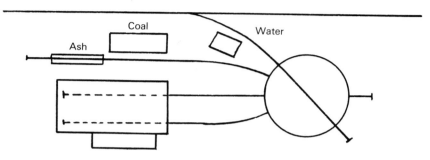

Larger dead-end type of shed with turntable.

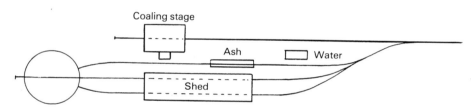

Through type of engine shed with turntable.

out your plan full size when you have reached what you think may be your final design. Lining paper used for wall-papering is cheap and convenient for this purpose. You will need a long ruler, a pencil, an eraser, and some templates for the radii you will be using — cut from card, hardboard or ply. It is usually most convenient to work on the floor. If you are planning to use Peco points you will find a set of the Peco point plans valuable. By working full size you can avoid errors that can easily arise in small scale plans.

N scale

In general the principles of planning in N scale are similar to those for 00 scale with an appropriate reduction in dimensions, but there are a few special points to bear in mind. As the majority of published track plans are designed for 00 or HO scale it may well be that the modeller will wish to adapt such a

plan for N scale. As a rough guide we can halve the linear dimensions reducing the area to a quarter. However, a direct conversion in this way may be neither possible nor desirable. The size of the operator is, of course, the same no matter what the scale of the layout, thus if there is a central operating well or some access openings it will probably be impossible to reduce the size of these. However, as the overall dimensions will be greatly reduced, while the operator's reach remains the same, the whole of the layout may now be accessible from any of the edges allowing the modeller to operate from one side instead of from the central well, which can then be covered with scenery. If a central wall is retained the layout size cannot be reduced as much but if you have enough space it is worth while keeping the well. The layout will appear more realistic if viewed and operated from the centre as only part will be visible at any one time making the round and round nature of the line, if a continuous run design, much less apparent.

It is often undesirable to reduce an 00-scale plan to quarter size for N scale; the resulting appearance is likely to be very disappointing with a much more toy-like effect than if it had been built in the larger scale. This is because the actual size of the layout is so much smaller and the eye sees so much more of it at a single glance. This is aggravated by the fact that the viewing position remains the same height above the layout, and is now twice as high in proportion. If you measure out a 6 ft × 4 ft rectangle and a 3 ft × 2 ft rectangle and compare them you will get some idea of this effect. If there is an oval, its continuous design is more obvious than in the original size. Things can be improved a little by building the layout higher from the ground so that you do not look down on it as much, but if possible it is better to reduce the linear dimensions only to about three-quarters of the 00 size rather than to half. This will allow the use of larger radius curves and give a generally less cramped appearance.

Another point which must be considered is the clearance for raised tracks crossing over low level tracks beneath. As the track base thickness will probably be the same as for 00 scale and as the same or greater clearance in actual terms will be required, the clearances cannot be reduced proportionally with the other dimensions. This will mean that an increase in the gradient will be needed for the N-scale layout. This is another reason for reducing the layout size by less than the full half.

If you have a larger space available but are thinking of N scale rather than 00 to allow you to build a more extensive and interesting model railway it is essential not to be too ambitious. We have become used to thinking of an 00-scale layout of say 8 ft × 4 ft as being within the capabilities of a beginner and it may be tempting to think of an N-scale layout in the same area. If the track plan is kept simple with not too many points, and emphasis is more on sweeping curves, gentle gradients and realistic landscape, this may be very successful. However, it is likely to be disastrous if an attempt is made to use the space for an N-scale version of a complex 16 ft × 8 ft 00-scale layout designed for a group of advanced modellers! This may be an exaggeration but it is very easy to get carried away with enthusiasm in the circumstances and some restraint is needed.

The fact that a 180° turn can be made in N scale (in as little as 20 in of baseboard width) creates some possibilities not open to the modeller working in 00 scale. For example, on a branch line terminus to fiddle yard scheme it is possible in N scale to include a reversing loop with some hidden sidings arising from it in place of the usual fiddle yard, making operation more convenient. Similarly, loops can be fitted at each end of a long, narrow layout to make it a continuous run design without making the layout too wide to be fitted along a wall or two walls of a room.

Eight Oaks station on a British N (1:48) scale layout built by Bob Jones. In N scale, platforms long enough to look realistic can be provided without needing a large space.

Structures

The structures on a model railway layout are a very important part of the landscape. Not only do they add scenic interest but in some cases they also provide extra operational possibilities for the line by creating traffic. For the best effect, both for individual buildings and for the overall appearance of the layout some planning in the selection and positioning is essential. Any temptation to just rush out to the local model shop once the track is down and to buy whatever takes the eye, or happens to be in stock at the time, is to be resisted!

In some cases a structure model needs to be planned accurately at an early stage. For example, the beautifully modelled machine shop on Mike Sharman's period layout is an integral part of the layout design so its size and position, and the position of the tracks, standard, narrow and broad gauge, entering it all had to be decided before the track laying was carried out. In other situations it may be important to plan ahead to ensure that there will be sufficient space for a particular model building, and that the sidings will be suitably positioned in relation to it. This will give a more realistic result than merely making the structures fit in later with the tracks already in place. The dimensions of model buildings constructed from the kits of some manufacturers are listed in their catalogues and this can be useful in advance planning.

We can divide model railway structures into three main groups, the railway buildings, such as stations, goods sheds, engine sheds and so on; buildings associated with the railway and providing traffic for it, factories, mines, warehouses, etc and incidental buildings in the landscape, houses, farms, hotels, garages, shops, and so on.

There is a good range of model buildings, mostly in kit form, available commercially in 00/HO and N scales, and these can often be easily modified or converted to suit your requirements more closely and to give you some individuality for your layout. Another popular technique is the combination of parts from two or more kits, known as cross-kitting, to make larger or different structures.

The greatest choice and scope, of course, comes with scratch-building structures for your layout. A good selection of materials is stocked by model shops including brick, stone and tile papers, balsa, plastic and corrugated copper.

Whether you use kits or construct your own buildings from scratch you should choose prototypes appropriate to the locality in which your railway is supposed to be set and to the type of railway you are modelling. The architectural style and details and the construction material used — wood, brick or stone — are often characteristic and the right selection can do much to make your layout appear authentic.

Most of us have space for only a small layout and beginners should start modestly even if there is plenty of room available, hence there is space for only relatively few buildings so we should be quite selective. Each should be worth its place on the layout and must add to the interest and overall appearance. We need buildings with character which will fit in with each other and generally they should be fairly small as large structures may tend to dwarf the rest of the layout. Buildings with interesting or irregular lines, with varying textures due to the use of several different materials such as brick, stone, wood, corrugated iron, and with additions, alterations and repairs over the years, together with the effects of weathering, often make good modelling subjects. Generally I find the older buildings more attractive in model form than the new modern structures. Remember that on a layout the view point is almost always from above and roofs are particularly noticeable. Thus buildings with varied rooflines due to gables and dormers, and with interesting chimneys and other roof details are especially suitable for modelling purposes.

Just as important as the selection of which structures will make good individual models

These low relief warehouses at the rear of the industrial layout built by Allan Sibley and Brian Dorman complete the scene and also conceal a fiddle yard.

This superbly detailed railway workshop on Mike Sharman's period layout is an important feature of the railway. Note the three different track gauges inside the building with, from the front, broad-, narrow- and standard-gauge tracks.

is the choice and arrangement to form a visually effective grouping. This takes a bit of practice and experience but can make all the difference in the final appearance. Develop a sense of arrangement by studying groupings which you find visually appealing—both in pictures of prototype structures and of layouts built by the expert scenic modellers

and shown in the model press—and try to decide why they look good. Experiment with separate models, putting them in various positions in relation to one another until you find the best arrangement. You will soon learn how to achieve a good effect on your layout. In general avoid very regular patterns with straight streets and buildings in orderly

Structures

56

The arrangement of the structures in this attractive 00-scale display layout featuring Builder Plus kits has been planned to create a realistic model town and the railway blends naturally into the scene.

rows. More irregular arrangements are not only more typical of the prototype but will also make your layout appear larger.

A very effective technique where space is limited at the rear of a layout is the use of low relief structures. These are buildings with only the front wall and the front parts of the side walls and roof modelled while the rest is omitted. Although the models have a depth of only an inch or so they look correct from any viewing angle provided that other buildings, trees or other features are placed to conceal the lack of depth. The appearance is much more realistic than merely using a painted backscene. Some special kits are available for structures of this type, for example, the card kits made by Superquick and Hamblings, or alternatively you can use ordinary kits and employ the front and back separately as low relief models. If you prefer to scratch-build these models they are, of course, much quicker and easier to construct than conventional structures as only the front is fully modelled.

Structure models can also be utilised as scenic barriers to visually break up a length of track to make it appear longer, or to conceal part of an oval of track or a fiddle yard. Low relief structures near the back of the layout are especially useful in covering hidden tracks, storage sidings or a fiddle yard. A row

of buildings along the centre of the baseboard, with or without a double-sided backdrop, can divide the layout into two separate towns making the railway seem longer and the stations further away from each other.

There are a number of kits available now for structures which are motorised. These include windmills with moving sails, water-mills fitted with small pumps so that real water can be circulated to turn the wheels, factories with moving conveyor belts and so on. Though some modellers may feel that these are rather gimmicky they are well worth considering, particularly on a small layout where any extra movement which can be introduced, in addition to the trains, will add to the interest of the scene. There are also some excellent working crane models for dock and goods yard use.

You may like to include on your layout two linked industries, between which there is rail traffic—for example, a mine from which ore is taken to a processing plant. For the most realistic effect the wagons in trains from the mine should be loaded with ore, while trains of empty wagons run back from the processing plant to the mine. To avoid the task of loading and unloading by hand many modellers ignore the inaccuracy and run full and empty wagons indiscriminately. However, a neat scheme to allow correct running

Model Railway Guide 2

Many excellent industrial structures are available in kit form so it is easy to provide an interesting variety for a layout. Although the Continental kits are in HO or Continental N scale they can be used satisfactorily for 00- and British N-scale layouts respectively. This well detailed model is the Kibri HO-scale Large Gravel Silo.

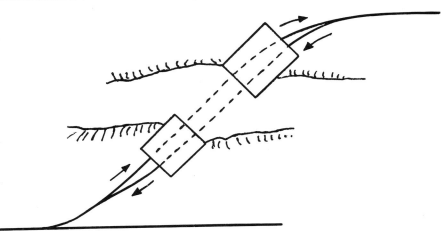

This arrangement allows empty wagons to enter the mine and full ones to leave it, while at the processing plant the reverse occurs, without the need for any loading or unloading of wagons.

has been devised by some modellers. The two industries are positioned either side of a ridge of hills, a row of industrial buildings or a double sided backdrop and hidden tracks connect them as shown in the diagram. Thus full wagons pushed into the processing plant are removed from the mine (and conversely empty wagons pushed into the mine are pulled out) at the other end of the hidden track from the processing plant.

Structures

Scenery

There is often a tendency for the modeller to concentrate on the designing of a track plan which will provide interesting operation, on the laying of smooth track for good running and on the correct wiring of the track. Once satisfied with these aspects he then adds scenery very much as an afterthought. Unfortunately such scenic work often appears unnatural and contrived. This is a pity because scenery can do a great deal to make a layout more realistic and interesting. Good scenic work not only makes the layout more attractive but also makes it look larger than it actually is. The scenery can also help to disguise such operationally necessary features as sharp curves, hidden tracks and fiddle yards. It can also be used to emphasise features we wish to show up.

It is important to plan the scenery in a general way with the track plan. Do not worry about the smaller details at this stage, as there will almost certainly be minor changes you wish to make during construction. In the prototype the landscape is, obviously, there before the railway which is planned to run through it. In the model the scenery is added last, but we should try to make it look as if it were there first. We must consider the type of terrain we want to model (hilly or flat, rural or urban) and the placing of a river, lake or canal. If your model is to be set in a particular location it is worth while visiting the area to see what the landscape is like. Make sketches or take photographs to guide you later when you are working on your layout.

By building up the scenery in the central part of this small 00-scale layout Terry Jenkins has created a dividing barrier between the two sides of the layout helping to conceal the oval track plan and making the layout more realistic.

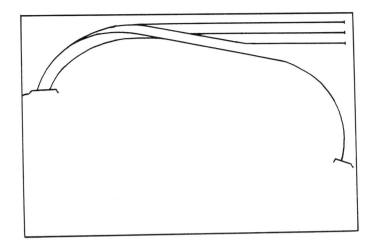

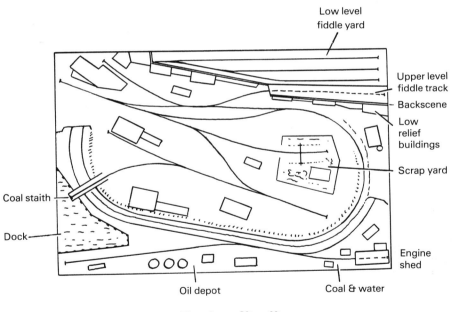

00 scale   6ft × 4ft

This industrial layout is also a development of the basic oval and again uses Hornby or Airfix points (one Hornby curved point is employed). The low level tracks are laid first and the layout can be operated at this stage. Later the modeller can construct the upper level and the track leading up to it. There is great scope for structure modelling and for scenic detailing and the operating potential is also good if you enjoy shunting. Trains of wagons are brought from the hidden sidings at the rear of the oval and up to the high level where the wagons are distributed to various industries including a scrap yard and a coal staith which passes above the low level tracks to load barges at the dock. Use of one of the card order schemes for deciding which wagon must go to which siding will add to the operating interest. The traffic will be mainly goods but you can also run an occasional workmen's train.

A model of the layout

64

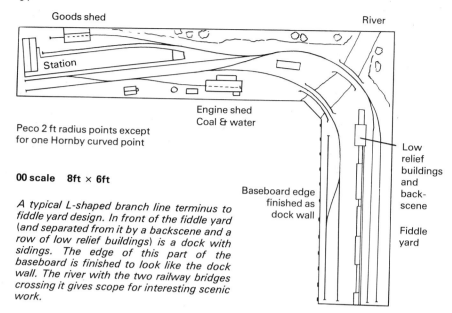

Goods shed

Station

River

Engine shed
Coal & water

Peco 2 ft radius points except
for one Hornby curved point

00 scale   8ft × 6ft

*A typical L-shaped branch line terminus to
fiddle yard design. In front of the fiddle yard
(and separated from it by a backscene and a
row of low relief buildings) is a dock with
sidings. The edge of this part of the
baseboard is finished to look like the dock
wall. The river with the two railway bridges
crossing it gives scope for interesting scenic
work.*

Baseboard edge
finished as
dock wall

Low
relief
buildings
and
back-
scene

Fiddle
yard

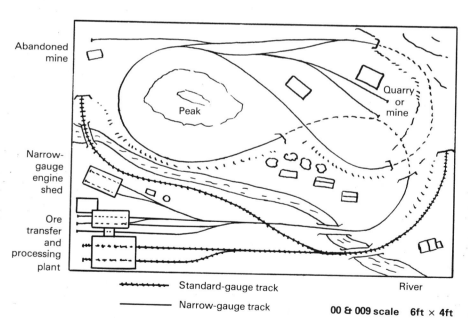

Abandoned
mine

Peak

Quarry
or
mine

Narrow-
gauge
engine
shed

Ore
transfer
and
processing
plant

++++++ Standard-gauge track

———— Narrow-gauge track

River

00 & 009 scale   6ft × 4ft

*A simple dual-gauge 00/009 layout. The standard-gauge oval with sidings can be laid first and
the layout can be operated in this form until the modeller wishes to add the narrow gauge. The
hidden standard-gauge tracks have been omitted from the plan for clarity, they merely
complete the oval though hidden sidings can also be included if desired. The narrow gauge is
an out and back design and the reversing loop requires special wiring. The dual-gauge
crossing is a Liliput product. The standard-gauge points are Hornby or Airfix.*

Model Railway Guide 2